Ethnologia Europaea

Journal of European Ethnology

Volume 36:1
2006

MUSEUM TUSCULANUM PRESS · UNIVERSITY OF COPENHAGEN

Copyright © 2007 Ethnologia Europaea, Copenhagen
Printed in Sweden by Grahns Tryckeri AB, Lund 2007
Cover and layout Pernille Sys Hansen
Cover photo www.taptrappers.nl, Woerden
ISBN 978 87 635 0691 5
ISSN 0425 4597

This journal is published with the support of the Nordic board for periodicals in the humanities and social sciences.

Museum Tusculanum Press
University of Copenhagen
Njalsgade 126
DK-2300 Copenhagen S
www.mtp.dk

CONTENTS

Anne Eriksen
The Murmur of Ruins. A Cultural History   5

Viktoriya Hryaban
Casting Post-Socialist Memory. Monuments and
Memorials as Instruments of Identity Politics in the Ukraine   21

Hilje van der Horst
Turkish Lace. Constructing Modernities and Authenticities   32

Stijn Reijnders
Holland on the Slide. Celebrating the Nation on Television   45

Silke Meyer
The Germans as the *Alter Ego* of the English?
The German Doctor in Eighteenth-Century Debate   58

THE MURMUR OF RUINS
A Cultural History

Anne Eriksen

> What is the difference between a ruin and a badly maintained building? The question can hardly be answered, for what defines ruins is not material decay in itself, but a specific understanding of it. Today, the message of ruins appears obvious: Ruins are predictably fascinating, romantic and picturesque. This romanticism is not timeless, but has its own cultural history. The murmur of ruins is the speech of modernity and the modern conception of time and history. It is about the development of a thoroughly modern subjectivity, centred on the emotionally competent individual, and the ethical values associated with this kind of personality and personal authenticity.
>
> *Keywords:* ruins, historicity, romanticism, cult of sensibility, heritage

What is the difference between a ruin and a poorly maintained building? Is it a matter of age, the ruin has to be old? Or is it the degree of decay, a ruin is a building lacking its roof? Perhaps the core of the question is the method and materials of construction – wooden buildings do not become ruins? There is hardly a definitive answer to this question, but perhaps what is more to the point is that it may not even be very relevant. What defines a ruin is not the material decay itself, but a specific understanding of it. The ruin is the product of a certain kind of discourse, a way of ascribing value and meaning to certain kinds of decay. This discourse has become so natural that it seems to stem from the ruin itself, it appears to be uttered by the ruin itself with its own voice. Moreover, the utterances frequently are about nature or natural processes: the ruin is on its way back into nature. It is part of the landscape and of its surroundings in other ways than normal, well-kept buildings are. Contrary to other edifices, the ruin is not a thing, an artefact, *in nature,* but an organic *part of* nature. The ruin also speaks about the past, about what once was but is no more – i.e. about the nature of time and the perishability of all things. Even here the process of naturalization is at work, relating the message of the ruin to organic and thereby natural processes of life and death.

Nonetheless, the voices of the ruins are not their own. Their speech does not emanate from their stones, bricks and mortar, but from history and from the cultural context of the spectator. The meaning of the ruins is created through the application of a certain kind of reader competence, the use of a culturally and historically defined schema of coding and decoding. The aim of this article is to look into some aspects of the cultural history of this discourse.

Today, the message of ruins is easily understood, it appears obvious and simple. Ruins are fascinating, romantic, picturesque and enigmatic in very predictable ways. They are easily read, their language is clear, and the moods and emotions they create are well-known and well-established. Most of us know what to feel, think and say at the sight of a ruin. Elements of mystery and enigma are integrated parts, but even they follow well-defined patterns and are easily decoded. Ruins are part of popular culture and staple elements of what may be called popular romanticism. In one of her novels, Jane Austen describes the joy of the heroine, Catherine Morland, who has been invited to visit some friends at Northanger Abbey. The manor has been constructed over the remnants of a medieval abbey, and with delightful shudders, Catherine anticipates the most interesting experiences:

> Its long, damp passages, its narrow cells and ruined chapel, were to be within her daily reach, and she could not entirely subdue the hope of some traditional legend, some awful memorials of an injured and ill-fated nun (Austen 1818/1976: 918).

The background for Catherine's dreams is her favourite literature, the Gothic novels to which she constantly refers. In these narratives, ruins are the self-evident place for gruesome events and the clue to terrible secrets. Catherine fantasizes herself into the role of a Gothic heroine, and is deeply disappointed when Northanger Abbey proves to be a modern, comfortable and well-maintained country house. Her feverish dreams of damp passages, secret messages and awful crimes among the ruins sadly come to nothing. Austen's novel was published in 1818, indicating that by then ruin romanticism was so well-established that she both could make it an object of irony and use it to depict a sentimental and somewhat silly young girl. Austen's text builds on the presupposition that the language of ruins is known to her readers, who will be able to understand the irony. At the same time, Catherine's awakening from her world of dreams, ruins and romantic clichés is a central part of her development, transforming her from a sentimental and naive girl into a mature woman (Austen 1818/1976: 903).

Nevertheless, ruin romanticism is not timeless. The ruins' speech is that of a historically specific mentality: It is the speech of modernity and of a modern conception of time and history. This also means that the ruins' message is not one of eternal truth about the universally human, but rather must be seen as the creation of specific historical conditions and a certain way of thinking about time and human life. If ruins also had a voice in earlier periods, they spoke other languages and conveyed other messages.

In his anthology *Le Temps en Ruines,* the French ethnologist Marc Augé says that "the future will not create ruins – it does not have time for it" (Augé 2003/2004: 137). He describes how late-modern societies generate "non-places" (*non-lieux*) like airports, motorways, industrial zones and slums in the peripheries of great cities. When buildings and plants in such places are abandoned or collapse, they do not become ruins, they become witnesses to destructive social and economic systems: "The rubble of recent times and the ruins born by the past do not resemble each other. There is a fundamental difference between the historical time of destruction, which reveals the madness of history (the streets of Kabul or Beirut), and pure time, 'the time in ruins', the ruins which have lost history or that history has lost" (Augé 2003/2004: 135). The real ruins, those left by former times, bear witness to time that moves slowly and to natural processes taking their time. They invite reflections and musings about eternal and existential questions that never lose their relevance. According to Augé such ruins represent "pure time", time that has evaded history and evolved into nature (Augé 2003/2004: 34ff).

Like so many other critical theories of modernity and modernisation, Augé's reflections have a romantic base. They are founded on ideas about rupture and a loss of meaning, and about a "before" when this rupture had not yet occurred and fragmentation not yet set in. Nonetheless, this idea about "before" is a systematic rather than a historic category; it is the logical opposition of modernity rather than its historical predecessor. The historian Mark S. Phillips points to the same logic in his discussion of the notion of tradition. Frequently used as a general name for the state of things before modernisation, tradition is understood "as a point of origin, rather than a process". In modernisation theory, this implies that "since tradition matters primarily for its contrastive value, it is always modernity, not traditionality, that requires specific analysis" (Phillips 2004: 17). The contrastive perspective built into these theories implies that tradition always will be presented as that which modernity is *not*, and correspondingly that tradition itself is never – really – made the object of analysis. The presentation thus is just seemingly historical, and, what is more serious: the contrastive approach may cover up more profoundly historical matters. In relation to ruins, what is at stake here is the understanding of time and the past, the experience of historicity. Augé's theories do not consider that the idea of "pure time", or at least the idea of contemplating it with respect to ruins, may be as modern as the airports and industrial plants of his contrastive model.

Even if the original buildings may be old and the ruins they have left are the products of organic processes in time that moves slowly, the meaning that is read into these ruins is neither universal nor timeless. The ideas of "pure time" versus history are specific to modernity, invariably linked to an understanding of time as linear, and of history as temporalized (Koselleck 1985). Jane Austen's heroine expresses her ideas about ruins less elegantly and in less philosophically sophisticated ways than Marc Augé. Indeed, her dreams are centred more on expectations of delightful shudders and interesting experiences than on theoretical reflections about time and human knowledge. However, their ideas both belong to the same – modern – way of thinking: ruins speak a natural language. They tell tales about a time that is past, lost and irreparably out of reach, but which still concerns the present world in fundamental ways. Be it the delightful shudder, the disclosure of forgotten and deep secrets or – more philosophically – insight into existential questions, the logic is the same: by listening to the ruins, living humans can acquire an understanding of the fundamental conditions of their own lives, their own existence, their own present.

In our world, this ruin romanticism is a matter of course and a truism. It is expressed in a number of genres and contexts, and serves as the foundation for classics like Rose Macaulay's *Pleasure of Ruins*, originally published in 1953 and later issued in a number of reprints and new editions. A much acclaimed new-comer on the same scene is Christopher Woodward's *In Ruins* from 2001. In both cases, the timelessness of the ruins' "melancholy grandeur" is taken as a given, both by the authors and their reviewers. The same applies when ruins are defined as cultural heritage and tourist attractions, and "romantic ruin" appears as a separate antiquarian category (e.g. searching "ruin" at http://www.english-heritage.org.uk). Such monuments are frequently used as scenes for historical plays, knight tournaments and other kinds of historical reconstructions – and just as frequently become a source of conflict between the antiquarian authorities in charge of conservation, on the one hand, and the enthusiastic players and their audiences on the other. What is at stake is the right to interpret and enjoy the ruins. Are they to be scenes of plays and performances, or historical source material – or just aesthetic objects to be contemplated at a distance? The conflicting views hardly ever relate to the *meaning* of the ruins. Uncontestedly, they remain the venerable carriers of fascinating, valuable and deeply meaningful messages from the past. Perhaps less conventionally, ruin romanticism also finds expression in such activities as so-called urban exploration, defined as "a kind of amateur expedition of discovery in urban settings. Old industrial plants, abandoned hospitals, sewers, air raid-shelters and tunnels have attracted this kind of interest" (Willim 2005: 153, my translation). Analysing this kind of "alternative tourism", Robert Willim sees the attraction of such expeditions in an understanding of the constructions and plants as ruins. He says that "in the exploration of abandoned sites, for example industrial ruins, various emotions may be aroused. The excitement of being in a forbidden place may awaken feelings of melancholy or reflections on changeability and the transitoriness of all things" (Willim 2005: 154). The abandoned constructions of urban modernity are thus ascribed the same symbolic meaning and the same potential for emotional experiences as more "regular" ruins – for example those at Northanger Abbey.

The Origins of Ruin Romanticism

Ruin romanticism was born in the eighteenth century. As a literary phenomenon it is closely related to the churchyard poetry of the same period, and on a more general level to aesthetic theories of the sublime as well as the picturesque (e.g. Fehrman 1956). In his broad presentation of the ruin motif in Western painting, the art historian Michel Makarius demonstrates how the motif and its meanings have changed over time. In Renaissance painting ruins frequently occur in nativity scenes and pictures presenting the adoration of the Magi. The stable is painted as the ruins of a classical building, with columns, arches, cornices and ornaments. Makarius shows that these pictorial elements serve several functions. They bear witness to Renaissance rediscovery of antiquity and the admiration for classical culture, but they also work as an allegory of heathendom defeated by Christianity. The decayed or collapsed buildings create a contrast to the new life and salvation promised by the Child. Within this complex, the Eastern Magi represent a third tradition of knowledge, in addition to Christianity and pre-Christian heathendom: the Orient (Makarius 2004).

Even if these scenes convey an understanding of historical phases and change, their idea of history differs from that of romanticism. These ruins do not speak about the passing of (linear) time, of the insignificance of human beings and the perishability of all worldly things. Their message is far more specific, about how different "reigns" and traditions follow each other according to a divine plan. The pictorial

Ill. 1: One of very few Norwegian contributions to ruin romanticism was supplied by the vestiges of the medieval cathedral of Hamar, which became part of the romantic garden at Storhamar manor. The artist J. Frich drew the ruins in 1848.

elements – be they oriental Magi or classical columns – do not refer to some otherwise unspeakable level of meaning concerning eternal, existential questions, but are specific indexical signs of the various traditions involved.

During the Renaissance and afterwards, ruins meant classical ruins, remnants of buildings from Greek and Roman antiquity. The voice that is associated with them correspondingly is related to the dominant view of antiquity, above all the ideas of the classical representing something very different from a historical epoch in the modern sense of the word. Instead, antiquity was seen as a pattern and an ideal, the realisation of values of timeless worth and validity raised high above the fleeting changeability of human life and human history. In this context, ruins did not speak of transitoriness in the more general sense, rather their discourse was about the loss of the perfect form and perfect beauty of classical art and architecture. But the ruins also demonstrated how classical art maintained its greatness even when destroyed. In them, the giants of the past were speaking to the dwarfs of the present. This was not, moreover, the discourse of the irreparable and deeply existential loss so often portrayed in modernisation theory, but rather an urgent appeal to emulate the past and the ancients, to once again strive towards the same degree of perfection and beauty.

The meaning of ruins as pictorial elements changed during the eighteenth century, above all because the ruin now appeared as an autonomous aesthetic object and became a topic of independent aesthetic reflections. In 1765, the *Encyclopédie* defined "ruin" as a pictorial genre:

> Ruin is a term in painting for the depiction of almost entirely ruined buildings: 'beautiful ruins'. The name 'ruin' is applied to a picture representing such ruins. 'Ruin' pertains only to palaces, elaborate tombs, or public monuments. One should not talk of 'ruin' in connection with a rustic or bourgeois dwelling; one should then say 'ruined buildings' (English version from Makarius 2004: 81).

The text points out that a ruin is not any decayed building but that the term refers to an artistic presentation of certain *kinds* of decayed and partly destroyed constructions. They are no longer explicitly classical, but still have to have a certain grandeur.

The aesthetics of ruins found in the *Encyclopédie* was developed by Diderot and closely related to the ideas of the sublime (Makarius 2004: 81f). The sublime, understood as a transcendental experience of greatness was originally related to the appreciation of dramatic natural scenes and natural forces: mountains (above all the Alps), glaciers, volcanoes, maelstroms, thunderstorms, even earthquakes. In his essay "A Philosophical Enquiry into the Origin of Our Ideas of the Sublime and Beautiful" from 1756, the philosopher Edmund Burke argued that the sublime and the beautiful were mutually exclusive: beauty is that which pleases us, while the sublime has the power to compel and destroy. Makarius describes the sublime as a play between the attractive and the repulsive: "The sublime ought thus to be understood as the estetic and psychological expression of a fundamental principle: man and nature are subjected to conflicting *forces*" (Makarius 2004: 84, italics in original). He refers to the philosopher Georg Simmel who points out that this principle is demonstrated in the ruin, which unites two opposite forces. On the one hand is man's "will to erect buildings on the principle of verticality; on the other, nature tends to erode or flatten them" (Makarius 2004: 84).

Diderot's poetics of ruins is above all developed in his texts on art criticism, published as *Ruines et paysage, Salon de 1767* (Bukdahl et al. 1995). His point of departure is paintings – "ruins" as the genre is defined in the *Encyclopédie* – by the French artist Hubert Robert, who came to be known as *Robert des Ruines*. Compared to earlier years, Diderot here develops new methods for his criticism. Mixed with his description and evaluation of each work, he now presents more general reflections on philosophical and aesthetic questions (Bukdahl 1995: 5ff). The method is extensively applied to the discussion of Robert's pictures, where Diderot "sketches a poetics of ruins with far more wide-reaching perspectives than those intended by the artist himself" (Bukdahl

1995: 10, my translation). He is correcting Robert because the paintings, according to his (Diderot's) view, contain too many figures and too many anecdotic genre scenes, saying "M. Robert, you do not yet know enough about why ruins give such pleasure, regardless of the varieties of accidents they reflect". To explain himself, he exclaims: "The ruins arouse great ideas in me. Everything is shattered, everything perishes, everything passes. Only the world is lasting. Only time is lasting. How it is old, this world! I move between two eternities. Wherever I cast my glance, the objects that surround me announce an end [...]" (Diderot 1767/1995: 338, my translations).

Diderot's perspective turns the painting of ruins into a reflection upon basic conditions of human existence. Bukdahl underlines the close ties to Burke's discussions of the sublime, and shows that Diderot's poetics of ruins heralds the coming of German painter Caspar David Friedrich's works from the first decades of the next century (Bukdahl 1995: 12ff). Makarius on the other hand points to aspects of Diderot's poetics of ruin that have been highly influential in a more general context of cultural history: today, the texts from 1767 may appear commonplace, even kitschy. The "great ideas" aroused in Diderot have become common property, parts of popular romanticism, sentimental clichés. For this reason it may also be difficult to understand the full originality of Diderot's thinking, and to disregard the process of naturalization that his ideas have since been subject to. But just for this reason, because the ideas have gained such great acceptance and come to appear so self-evident, it is important to emphasize that Diderot's texts contributed heavily to transforming the ruins from more or less meaningful elements of scenery to autonomous philosophical and aesthetic objects (Makarius 2004: 111).

Makarius' presentation of ruins in Western pictorial art has a close parallel in Carl Fehrman's discussion of ruins in Western literature (1956). Like Makarius, Fehrman emphasizes the role of the ruin as the vanitas-motif in early romanticism. The ruin became a symbol of the futility and transitoriness of all human effort. Fehrman interprets this as the opposite of the preceding classicism and its cult of antiquity as a timeless ideal. Even if the ruins of early romanticism still were Greek or Roman, their meaning had changed. Their message was no longer centred upon the eternal ideals of classical culture and classical beauty, but came to treat more generally human, existential problems relating to life and death, time and transitoriness. But at the same time Fehrman emphasizes that this romantic interpretation itself underwent certain changes during the eighteenth century.

Returning from their *Grand Tour* through Europe to Italy, the Northerners, in particular the English, started to discover the medieval ruins of their own countries. For a long period of time such ruins had been seen as far too lacking in harmony, barbaric and irregular to be the objects of aesthetic reflections. But as classicism made way for romanticism, even the domestic "Gothic" ruins found their place in the aesthetic universe. In part, this was due to a re-evaluation of the Middle Ages as a historical epoch, in part due to the new romantic aesthetics and its preference for the irregular, the incomplete and the fragmentary. Fehrman underlines that ruins no longer were just sublime, they might also hold a position within the other important category of romantic aesthetics: The ruin was the picturesque fragment incarnate (Fehrman 1956: 85ff).

Medieval ruins became a favoured element in poetry and painting, but also a much sought after blessing in fashionable gardens. Even though England was well supplied with ruins of medieval abbeys and chapels – like the ones Catherine Morland hoped to encounter at Northanger Abbey – the new romantic garden architecture led to a demand that at times exceeded the supply. The ethnologist Tine Damsholt states that the highly popular "English gardens" of this epoch served to stage the individual as emotional subject, "as they were planned with the idea of arousing changing emotions and moods in the visitors. Specific kinds of scenery were linked to certain emotional effects, in such a way that a fixed repertoire of causal relationships between scenery and emotion was established" (Damsholt 2000a: 158, my translation). Ruins became part of this encoded language, in the same way as grottoes, pagodas, hermitages, temples, pavilions and different kinds of altars (e.g. of friendship), tombs and monuments. If medieval structures already were present, things were simple and the ruin was incorporated in the planning of the garden's paths and prospects. Less fortunate proprietors solved this problem by constructing sham ruins, in the same way as others installed artificial waterfalls, built grottoes and made empty graves surrounded by poplars and weeping willows (Fehrman 1956: 98f; Damsholt 2000a: 158).

It is not easy to discover how widespread the sham ruins actually were, among other things because the difference between them and other popular "fabriques", like hermitages, Gothic follies and so on, was not always so clear (Hunt 2004: 41f). But whatever the case, the sham ruins drew much attention and soon gained a position as the very symbol of an exaggerated cult of sensibilities, where the sentimental had become more important than the authentic. It might therefore be fair to point out that the garden ruins – sham or real – originally were elements in a discourse on sensibility and subjectivity that was different from that of later periods, and consequently that they were assessed according to other criteria. In the golden era of romantic gardens, the ruin was above all an aesthetic object. It should elicit certain – frequently rather well-defined – emotions and moods in the competent spectator. In the new gardens the ruin was lifted out of the painting or the poetry and placed in real scenery. The experience was no longer based solely on the reading of a poem or the contemplation of a picture, but on the spectator's own promenade along garden paths. The ruins gained a new materiality, while their enjoyment at the same time was connected to the bodily experience of wandering in the garden, appreciating the turns and twists of the picturesque paths, and the joy of unexpected views. These experiences were prepared for through the planning of the garden, but their realisation was wholly dependent on the spectator and his/her activity: The wandering was a prerequisite to interesting perspectives as well as strong emotions. What is evoked is the same aesthetic competence as in the enjoyment of poems and pictures, the same ability to be moved in specific ways by certain artistic expressions, and the same knowledge of a causal relationship between scenery and emotion. It was not as antiquarian, historian or mason that the spectator was supposed to appreciate the ruin, but as a sensitive and aesthetically competent subject. Referring to Foucault's theories on the constructions of subjectivity, Tine Damsholt describes the garden promenade as a *technology of the self,* i.e. "a way to improve oneself via the emotions aroused by the garden" (Damsholt 2000b: 29). The garden architecture was part of the romantic cult of sensibility and – not least – of its ethical dimensions, where strong emotions were seen as the expressions of a noble character. Training oneself to express strong emotions in the right way –for example by crying and demonstrating compassion – became an important part of the development of the ethical subject (Damsholt 2000b: 27). The literary critic Sophie Le Ménahèze also points out that this new kind of subjectivity, represented by the romantic garden, very explicitly was contrasted with the rigid feudalism and empty greatness associated with the traditional formal garden (Le Ménahèze 2001: 543). The two kinds of gardens thus became symbols of contrasting values and subjectivities.

Problems concerning the historical authenticity of the ruins, and the corresponding ridicule of ruins which only imitate this authenticity, only occur when the ruins are perceived as historical testimonies and sources. As long as the value of ruins was their ability to arouse emotions and initiate certain kinds of philosophical reflections, newly built ruins may be considered as genuine as others. Their authenticity does not come from their historical source value, but is rather an aspect of the spectator's emotions and the noble character thus expressing itself. The authentic ruin then is the one able to produce authentic – strong – emotions.

Fehrman also analyses another aspect of the growing interest in medieval ruins: They were domestic and – to an increasing degree – perceived as national. Through them, ruin romanticism was transformed into a national past. The trend was particularly strong in the German states, and was manifested during the nineteenth century. Fehrman writes:

The ruin-like, the sentimental melancholy cedes the place. National, historic and heroic associations are evoked. The national current in German romanticism transforms the ruin in the direction of the heroic: it becomes a symbol of heroic times and heroic deeds (Fehrman 1956: 97, my translation).

This nationalization implied historicity, but history was understood in heroic terms. The ruins no longer bore witness to the transitoriness of all things, but rather to the heroism of the past. The more general symbolism of *vanitas* was supplanted by a more specific iconography of national history. Through its sheer material existence, the ruin in a very concrete way bore witness to national power and splendour – even if far in the past. The timeless validity of classical virtue was replaced by a demonstration of national character and national history. Ruins no longer called for an imitation of classical ideals, but for a re-birth of national virtue and national deeds – the deeds of one's *own* ancestors, the greatness of one's *own* past. The link between past and present was no longer provided by the general exemplarity of the classical age, but by the organic bonds between forefathers and heirs. The challenge was no longer to imitate but to inherit and pass on. Ruins were cultural heritage. Due to this transformation, ruins became one of numerous elements in the project of cultural nation building, a process taking place over large parts of the Western world during the nineteenth and twentieth centuries. The ruin no longer was "a concept of the pictorial arts", as stated by the *Encyclopédie*; it represented national history and supported national claims to power and influence.

With historization also came the establishment of modern antiquarian authorities, even this usually within national frames. National history and national culture supplied the arguments for conserving and restoring ruins and other antiquities. Taking care of them meant preserving the national past; gaining knowledge about them correspondingly meant gaining knowledge about the nation. Alongside museums and national archives, the antiquarian institutions played an important part in the construction of national cultures. The ruins were inscribed in a national discourse, and their aesthetic value subjected to national aims. This also created an additional message. The ruin not only requested the present to emulate the heroes of the past. Conserving, restoring and investigating the ruins became praiseworthy in itself, an heroic activity worthy of comparison with the deeds of the past. The white knights of the ruins were no longer the poets or the painters, but antiquarians or historians.

The Antiquarians' World

But where had the antiquarians been in the meantime? The ruins became autonomous aesthetic objects long before they acquired meaning as material remains with inherent value and a history of their own. Renaissance rediscovery of the classical world led to a degree of interest in its material vestiges. Classical buildings and fragments were investigated as models for contemporary architecture, but this did not involve any real interest in the ruins as such, what was important was the constructions they once had been. Moreover, the investigation did not lead to attempts at conservation or preservation of what was still left. In medieval Rome, ancient buildings had been adapted to fresh usage. Classical buildings had been transformed into Christian churches, or into castles and dwellings. The Pantheon was made into a church as early as 608, a fact that probably saved it from being ruined. The Colosseum was made a church by Benedict the 14th in the eighteenth century, and in the nineteenth century, the theatre of Marcellus still was owned by the Orsini family, who used it like a block of flats. The increased amount of construction work during the Renaissance period also led to another kind of "recycling": The older buildings served as quarries for the new. The Palazzo della Cancelleria, perhaps the finest of Rome's Renaissance palaces, is said to be made from marble taken from the Colosseum. Admiration for classical architecture thus led to the consumption of the buildings rather than their preservation. Antiquity was a resource, supplying models for architecture as well as building material.

Erudite antiquarian work on the other hand was

focused more on the study of texts and inscriptions than on buildings or ruins. Fragments with inscriptions were much sought after in the same way as coins and medals. The critical work of the humanists had developed awareness about possible forgeries in documents and literary sources. Inscriptions seemed to be witnesses of another kind. In them, the past spoke directly. This approach meant that antiquarian work was above all philological, with identification as one of its main concerns: Erudite work aimed at connecting the monuments and buildings still to be seen with the persons and events known from literary sources. Inscriptions – on fragments, tombs, medals or coins – were some of the important means for achieving this.

Originally, antiquarian work meant investigations into the classical past, but gradually it also came to include the various "national pasts" of Northern Europe. The interest in ruins for their own sake was still not that great. In her book on British antiquarians in the 18th century, the historian Rosemary Sweet says that even if the ruins of abbeys and churches were seen both as powerful antiquities and important vanitas-symbols, as "objects of interest in terms of their physical appearance, they were of secondary importance". She also points out that "the language available to describe them was correspondingly limited. The preservation of the ruin was simply a means of ensuring that the intangible memory of those whose lives and devotion it commemorated were saved from oblivion" (Sweet 2004: 242). Sweet further underlines that the buildings or ruins themselves rarely were used as the main sources of knowledge about their own history: "The materials with which ecclesiastical antiquaries worked were therefore primarily textual ones: the charters granted to monasteries, the endowment of churches, the epitaphs and inscriptions to be found within. The physical structure of the church itself was very much a secondary consideration" (Sweet 2004: 242). Ruins simply were demolished buildings. Their decay, and the transitoriness, could be lamented, but what could be more specifically gained from the buildings were still just fragments of knowledge about such things as genealogy. This also was the really important knowledge, worthy of being saved from oblivion. Apart from this, the physical remains of buildings were not of antiquarian interest.

Sweet's focus on the lack of terminology is also important in a Scandinavian context. In the Scandinavian languages Danish, Swedish and Norwegian, use of the word 'ruin' is comparatively recent and mostly to be found from the 19th century onwards. In older texts, the Latin word *rudera* is used, or the Nordic equivalents *levninger* (vestiges) or *rester* (remains). In these texts, the ruin is not yet a separate category, neither as physical monument nor as aesthetic object. Rudera is simply a matter of decayed or collapsed buildings. These vestiges are undefined in themselves, and are mentioned only as by-products of what they *have been*. Contrary to the ruins, rudera have no message other than that of decay, no voice of their own and no value proper to their present state.

Little attention has been paid to this discrepancy of meaning between the two terms ruin and rudera, neither in scholarly literature nor in translations of Latin texts: Rudera is normally translated as ruins, not as vestiges or remains. One example is the major work *Suecia antiqua et odierna*, originally published in the 1680s. It contains more than 350 plates, presenting ancient and recent Swedish castles, fortresses, churches, abbeys and so on, all supplied with short descriptions in Latin. In 1924 the texts were translated into modern Swedish. The Latin terms *ruderae*, *vestigiae* and *reliquiae* are all translated as *ruiner* (see *Suecia antiqua et odierna*). This means that the modern voice of the ruins is associated with a period when this voice had not yet been heard, and when the remains of old buildings still were nothing but silent vestiges. What has happened since is that the (modern) discourse of the ruins has become so self-evident and so seemingly inherent in their sheer masonry that their message also is being projected into the silent past.

A Nordic example of the kind of antiquarian work described by Sweet is Magnus Boraenius' dissertation on Vreta Abbey in Östergötland, a Swedish province. It was defended at the University of Uppsala in 1724, and is a work of a mere 48 pages in its modern edition. Just a little bit more than one of these pages is actually about the buildings at Vreta, the rest of the text examines, for example, the name of the abbey, its foundation and founders, the Cistercian Order, the properties and incomes of the abbey and – not least – the royal graves in the church. About the building, Borænius says that it is difficult to describe "as it shows itself in another form than before. In some way I shall still try to present it, even if it has been forsaken for so long a time" (Borænius 1724/2003: 19). According to Borænius, the building he is going to describe does not exist. What is left of it gives little information about what has been, and is not attributed independent value of any kind. A huge tree has grown up in the interior of the abbey, and Borænius uses it to argue that the roof of the building must be long gone – as it takes considerable time for a tree to grow so tall. Apart from this, the present state of the building does not make a point of departure for an analysis of its original plan or its history. Instead, Borænius has applied considerable energy to the study of documents related to the abbey, as well as to the study of inscriptions on the royal tombs. Both documents and inscriptions are reprinted in his thesis.

A number of greetings to the author on the occasion of his completed work are also included. They inform us clearly that what is important is not the physical remains of the abbey but rather the memories of past lives and devotion. The author's friend P. Ehrenpretz writes:

> You have taken on fresh efforts for the dead nuns of this place, by recounting their noble lives, the stately house, glorious temple, the monument of the kings, princes and nobles who are buried here, and who are particularly worthy of memory (Borænius 1724/2003: 13).

The antiquarian work is above all motivated by the wish to keep alive the memories of great men and women. According to his friends, this also is what constitutes the merit of Borænius' work. The same kind of argument is expressed in a greeting from the vicar of Vreta, Z. Z. Reuserus:

> How painful it is and how difficult to dig out of the hidden realms of history which seems to contribute to the honour of the Swedish and Gothic people, or to renew the memory of the ancient monuments. But the deed is equally beautiful and meritorious. In this way, models of virtue are veritably presented to our descendants, which they can imitate. The ancient monuments of our fatherland, seemingly overgrown with greenery and oblivion are restored to their former glory. They are fittingly brought to light and to the sight of the people, even those who have never before seen them with their own eyes (Borænius 1724/2003: 48).

History is about honour, glory and memory. The exemplarity of the past is underlined; it is a "model of virtue" for the present and the future to emulate. The argument links Borænius' antiquarian work to the tradition of exemplary historiography, where history worked as *magistra vitae* (Koselleck 1985: 21ff). According to this way of thinking, the real concern of history was to contribute to man's moral and political education, or – as Lord Bolingbroke wrote in his "Letters on the Study of History" from 1752: "History is philosophy teaching by examples" (from Jensen 2003: 113). What defined historical knowledge, then, was not its occupation with the past, but its exemplary character, and its primary task was to serve as a model for the present. This helps to make the actual, physical remains of buildings less important. The moral and religious messages of the past are the centre of interest, while broken masonry and decayed structures remain insignificant.

The absence of a terminology related to ruins is noticeable also in the answers to a questionnaire sent by the Government to all civil servants in Norway in 1743. These texts demonstrate clearly that the lack of terminology not only was accompanied by a lack of interest, but also led to a kind of invisibility: Even large ruins were treated as if they did not exist. The aim of the questionnaire was to gather material for an extensive, topographic description of the entire country, and the main focus was on natural resources and topics with economic implications. Nonetheless, some questions also concerned royal castles and fortresses, as well as "antiquities". In these answers, rudera is the common term for building remains. The respondents also frequently and vehemently stress that they write about decayed, demolished and abandoned buildings. For example, the church of the former abbey at Gimsøy in Southern Norway is said to contain the tombs of several noble persons, but we are also informed that the building "for a long time has been left to decay, and according to a decision by the late honourable *geheimeråd* Mr. Adaler is no longer in use. In its stead a pretty wooden building has been erected" (Røgeberg 2003: 68). This new, wooden chapel is mentioned by numerous civil servants of the region, and it is obvious that they see it as far more important than the remaining walls of the ancient building. As opposed to them, the new building was practically useful, functioning as the local chapel and therefore deserving of the words "pretty" and "stately". It also seems more important to report the meritorious deed of the noble Mr. Adaler than to describe the old monastery. It is this deed, not the walls of the ancient building, that is "historical", in the sense of exemplary. Mentioning the old walls and their decay serves above all to mark the contrast between the useless and the meritorious.

The large medieval castle in the city of Tønsberg, south of Oslo, also suffered from severe decay. It is described as "very ancient" and "destroyed", and had been ravaged by fire during the war against Sweden in 1503. The higher official (*stiftamtmann*) von Rappe writes that Tønsberg is

> ... the most ancient town of Norway and was in its time large and famous, but has been destroyed and reduced to ashes by the large fire that ravaged it more than 200 years ago, and in the centre of the town there has been a castle that was erected on a mountain which can be seen at the end of the town, and on the same mountain vestiges of the mentioned castle can still be seen (Røgeberg 2003: 56).

Even though Tønsberg is the oldest town in the country, and once has been both large and powerful, the ruins of the castle are not presented either as vanitas-symbol or as historic monument, but simply as rudera, vestiges, the remains of something that no longer exists – as "lime, bricks and stones" (Røgeberg 2005: 346). The installation has no practical use and its remains have not yet found a voice of their own. In this period, the vestiges of the medieval castle in Tønsberg consisted of a wide circular wall with remnants of numerous towers, in addition to the visible remains of three large brick and stone buildings. The hill where it is situated rises almost 80 meters above the city centre. But despite its size and dominant position, the castle remains practically invisible in the civil servants' answers to the questionnaire, it is barely mentioned. The vestiges did not belong to any clear-cut category and were not defined as interesting or meaningful, neither aesthetically nor relating to antiquarian work.

Even more invisible were the remains of the medieval cathedral of Hamar, in south-central Norway. The medieval town of Hamar had been abandoned, and the cathedral left as an enormous hill of gravel and rubble, out of which poked the arched top of the southern arcade. The bishop's castle, situated east of the church, was equally derelict, but parts of it had been put to use as a barn. Some of the buildings on the large farm, Storhamar, had also been built into the gravel heap that rose above them. Nevertheless, von Rappe says that "... the farm Storhamar [...] is situated at Hedemarck in the place where the town of Hamar once stood, of which no vestiges no longer remain" (Røgeberg 2003: 70). According to him, nothing is to be seen of the old glory. Today, around 250 years later, the ruins at Hamar are among the nation's most important historical monuments. To protect them, an enormous glass hall has been erected, solemnly inaugurated by the crown prince and several ministers in 1998.

Françoise Choay has analysed a development in the antiquarians' attitudes towards ruins during the eighteenth century. Parallel to the development in other branches of knowledge, in particular the natural sciences, new ideals came to dominate: knowledge must be based on observation. Literary tradition and the authority of classical texts no longer sufficed. For the antiquarian work this meant more field work and an extended use of maps and drawings. Among the consequences was a growing interest in how the buildings – or their remains – actually looked at the time of observation (Choay 1990: 60). But Choay also demonstrates that in spite of the new ideals, antiquarian drawings did not immediately present the buildings in their present state. The presentations also were formed by contemporary architectonical ideals and by the artists' own ideas on how the buildings once had looked. Not until the end of the eighteenth century did the drawings become precise, antiquarian registrations in a more modern sense.

Choay associates this development with changes in the notion of preservation, and says that "after nearly three hundred years of antiquarian work (i.e. from the renaissance onwards), the illustrated book still was the dominant form of conservation" (Choay 1999: 70, my translation). Rather than conserving actual buildings and other material remains from the past, the most important method for "preserving" buildings was the publication of large works of plates. *Suecia antiqua et odierna*, mentioned above, is one typical example. Thus it is obvious that what was important about ancient buildings was still their appearance, not their materiality. Through the drawings and plates, even huge buildings and installations could easily be presented in a well-preserved state, with the appearance they (at least according to the artist) once had had, and still "ought" to have; this was acknowledged as their real form. From this perspective, the ruins themselves still lacked interest.

Between Aesthetics and History

Carl Fehrman argues that it was seeing the real ruins of Italy that sparked European ruin romanticism, thereby establishing the ruin as an aesthetic category. At the same time, it appears that the ruin as antiquarian object and historical monument is heavily rooted in this romanticism. Not until the ruin was established as the object of aesthetic reflections did it appear as an antiquarian category. It was the artists, not the antiquarians who first listened to the voice of the ruins and sought to interpret their message. Poetry and painting contributed to the antiquarians' discovery, and helped them to see rudera as ruins. The aestheticizing of the ruins preceded their historization, and at the same time served as the necessary basis for interpreting the ruins as the valuable remains of a national past, and assigning the public authorities with the responsibility to take care of them.

However, the antiquarian and the aesthetic assessment of ruins were never completely identical. The antiquarians' monuments were not merely aesthetic objects, but also sources of knowledge, concrete traces of a historic past. The antiquarians' approach brought demands for research and claims for preservation. Furthermore, it also brought a new understanding of authenticity, no longer rooted in the emotions of the spectators, but in the materiality of the bricks and masonry. The ruins started to speak with forked tongues, creating contrasts that are still present today.

In 2006, the Norwegian antiquarian authorities launched their so-called "ruin-project", a grand-scale work of conservation of medieval ruins. On their website, the Directorate for Cultural Heritage (*Riksantikvaren*) demonstrates how the authorities' understanding of ruins is inscribed in a solid frame of laws and well-established procedures. "What is a ruin?" the Directorate asks, immediately supplying a very specific answer: It is the remains of a building or construction in stones or bricks in mortar, produced before the Reformation (1537) (*Ruinprosjektet*). Considered as a definition, the phrase seems rather odd, but the key to understanding lies in the context: According to Norwegian law, all medieval remains automatically are listed for protection. What is presented as a general definition of ruins on the website, is in reality a description of a specific antiquarian category, in this case even defined by law. This also implies that as long as it is medieval and in stone or brick, it does not matter *what kind* of building the ruin has been. The ruins do not have to be grand and monumental. The Directorate is even responsible for what it calls "invisible ruins", i.e. vestiges covered by earth. Analytically, such ruins may be seen as the purest incarnations of the antiquarian category. The aesthetic dimension is completely absent, but the "invisible ruin" is a historical source equal to all other remains of ancient masonry.

Nevertheless, the Directorate can not completely free itself from the multivocality of ruins, and the text goes on: "Ruins are not just physical remains. They also are mental monuments, telling us about knowledge, contacts, skills, spirituality, ideas, power relationships and politics. In this way, the ruins represent a part of our cultural treasury and our identity" (*Ruinprosjektet*). This interpretation reaches far beyond questions of mortar and bricks. Ruins are presented as a general cultural good. The aesthetic dimension is not in focus, but the references to "cultural treasury" and "identity" still create associations to the older vanitas-symbolism: Ruins bear witness to human life, to the passing of time, to knowledge about what and who we most fundamentally are.

The Swedish National Heritage Board *(Riksantikvarämbetet)* also appears to have a corresponding duality. The introduction to their website *Ruinportalen* (ruins' portal) states:

Ruins demonstrate the passing of time
Ruins are powerful and physically present symbols of time. They show that everything we humans have constructed, single buildings as well as entire societies and cultures, will weather away and be destroyed. The ruins also are enigmatic elements of our heritage: mystical fragments and elements of buildings difficult to understand, weathered and demolished parts, seemingly not interrelated. It contributes to the suggestive atmosphere of these sites that so much is left to our imagination *(Ruinportalen).*

Ruins are vanitas-symbols, they tell us about the passing of time and of the futility of all human effort. The ruins themselves, as well as these questions, are surrounded by a certain mystique, and this makes them an image of human conditions in a most fundamental way: We are all confronted with questions that are difficult to answer, and that is something each of us has to solve individually. These musings are accompanied by the following:

Whether the building really has to lack a roof to be considered a ruin, is subject to discussion. What happens to a ruin that is supplied with a roof to protect its walls? Is the ruin once again to be considered a building, and as such no longer listed and protected as a ruin? *(Ruinportalen)*.

The text goes on to argue that the notion of ruins must be extended and modernized. Even more recent constructions and less monumental buildings must be included, for example industrial plants or rural smallholdings, crofts and cabins. To explain the value of ruins, questions of the relationship between conservation and popularisation are important:

Ruin sites have great potential for events and experiences, but they also are important historical documents and an important part of our cultural heritage. Therefore they must be protected and guarded, and even used and brought to life *(Ruinportalen).*

In contemporary antiquarian and heritage work, events and spectacles on the one hand, and historical work and research on the other make a complicated network of conflict and cooperation. Events and experience are associated with popularisation, source value with protection and research. In their publications and on their websites, both the Swedish and Norwegian authorities comment on the tension between these two dimensions. Public use must consider the scientific value of the monument, and respect its need for protection and preservation. While antiquarian authorities must handle this duality on a practical level, it may more analytically be seen as a product of the composite origin of the ruin as an autonomous object. Modern antiquarian authorities are responsible for the care of constructions that are both *ruderae* and *ruins*. As ruderae they are the remains of past societies and cultures, and sources of scientific knowledge about this past. As such, they contain information about such things as social conditions, architecture, technology and mentality. As ruins they are also aesthetic objects, symbols of time and transitoriness, sources of wonder, imagination, dreams, a means of existential reflection. Both these ways of thinking about ruins are at the root of modern antiquarian work, but not always in harmony with each other.

The public debate on the preservation of the ruins of the medieval cathedral of Hamar will serve as a final example of how these two ways of thinking may conflict with each other, even when all parties involved wish to protect a monument generally regarded as highly valuable. After the Reformation in 1537, the cathedral of Hamar gradually fell out of use. It was heavily damaged by fire during the war against Sweden in 1567 and subsequently left to decay and "invisibility" (cf. above). Centuries later, a furnace for the production of lime was installed, consuming parts of the crumbled stonework. During the early decades of the nineteenth century, the ruin was "discovered" and put to use as a picturesque garden ruin. Antiquarian investigations were also undertaken. During the nineteenth and twentieth centuries the ruins, and in particular the tall southern arcade, have functioned as a symbol for the modern city of Hamar, and been one of the attractions of the local museum. In the 1980s the ruins were found to be in very bad condition. There was a great danger that the remaining masonry would crumble completely. A large glass shield was proposed as a cover over the entire original building,

Ill. 2: Hundred and fifty years have passed since Frich made his drawing of the ruins at Hamar. As a now highly cherished national monument, it has been built into a protective glass shield with its own aesthetic value. (Photo: Arthur Sand, University of Oslo.)

but due to funding problems this shield was not built until the late 1990s.

In the period from the discovery of the bad state of the ruins to the inauguration of the protective structure, a heated public debate raged at Hamar as well as in some of the national newspapers. The battle was fought between those who wanted the huge (and enormously costly) glass structure and those who did not. The adherents of the shield above all else saw the ruin as a historical source, as authentic medieval masonry with equally authentic traces of long historical processes. Referring to technical as well as antiquarian expertise they claimed that the shield, with its highly advanced technological solutions for controlling air and humidity, was the only way to preserve these values for posterity.

The opponents were of the opinion that the visual dimension and the specific relationship between ruin and landscape were the two important features of the ruin. Bearing this in mind, various conclusions were drawn. It was suggested that the ruin be repaired using new stones taken from the original quarry nearby. This solution was presented as "natural" both because it implied that all stones in the building would be the same kind of natural product, and because it would correspond with the traditional maintenance practice. Others meant that the weak parts of the ruin could be replaced by some modern, synthetic material – provided that it was not too visible. The most extreme point of view was to let the natural processes continue, even if this would finally mean the ruin's complete destruction (Eriksen 1999).

Both sides in this debate found the ruin to be an important local symbol, closely connected to a local feeling of belonging. The ruin was at the core of a historically based identity uncontested by both parties. On this point, the message of the ruin is unambiguous: it tells the inhabitants of Hamar who they are and where they belong. But apart from this, the fragments of the cathedral fed two rather different discourses.

The debate was interpreted as a conflict between local and popular interests, on the one hand, and national responsibility and scholarly attitudes on the other (Eriksen 1999). It was "the people" who propagated the open-air preservation of the ruins and who focused on the visual, the natural and the emotional. The experts, representing the museum and the antiquarian authorities, underlined source value, research and the authenticity of the cathedral's physical remains. But this article's investigations into the cultural history of ruins also demonstrate that the conflict may be seen in another and more far-reaching perspective. The supporters of the shield represent the more recent way of thinking, seeing the medieval walls both as rudera and ruin. The aesthetic dimension is not denied, but is combined with a historical mentality, connecting authenticity to the physical remains of the cathedral, not to the emotions aroused in the spectator. The opponents embraced the older poetics of ruins developed by Diderot and his contemporaries, seeing the ruin as an aesthetic category "arousing grand ideas", and as closely related to the ideas of the sublime, the transcendental experience of both joy and horror. Interpreted along these lines, it becomes clear that the debate not only was a struggle between local enthusiasts and national authorities, but that it was also a matter of different competences and mentalities. The arguments of the supporters were based on specialised professional knowledge (in part technological, in part historical). The opponents' point of view, on the other hand, presupposed a broader aesthetic competence, where a certain ability to respond emotionally to visual stimuli was at the core, and where authenticity is associated with the bonds between perception and character.

This short cultural history of ruins has attempted to show that even if ruins seem to convey a timeless message about the eternally human aspect, this message is actually quite recent, originating from the aesthetics of romanticism and its notions of the sublime and the picturesque. The self-evidence of this discourse in contemporary culture and intellectual life is in itself an indication of deeply romantic strands inherent in modernity and modern mentality. Even critical projects, such as the writings of Marc Augé, are influenced by this. Using this knowledge as a starting point, the study of ruins, or rather of the discourse ascribed to them, may contribute to an understanding of other, more fundamental questions concerning the cultural history of modernity. The discourse of ruins – or on ruins – is not just a monument to the cult of sensibility in romanticism. It is also about the development of a thoroughly modern subjectivity, centred on the emotionally competent individual, and about the ethical values associated with this kind of personality and personal authenticity. Furthermore, the interest in ruins is not just an accompanying example of the history of antiquarian work, it is also part of the development of the modern idea of historicity as a fundamental human condition.

References

Augé, Marc 2003, Italian edition 2004: *Rovine e macerie. Il senso del tempo*. Torino: Bollati Boringhieri.

Austen, Jane 1818/1976: *Northanger Abbey*. London: Hamlyn, Spring books.

Borænius, Magnus 1724: *Klostret i Vreta i Östergötland*. Translated from Latin to Swedish by K. Bergman 2003, Föreningen Klosterliv i Vreta, Linköping.

Bukdahl, Else Marie, Michel Delon & Annette Lorenceau (eds.) 1995: *Diderot. Ruines et paysages, Salon de 1767*. Paris: Hermann.

Bukdahl, Else Marie 1995: Diderot entre le 'modèle idéal' et 'le sublime'. In: Else Marie Bukdahl, Michel Delon & Annette Lorenceau (eds.), *Diderot. Ruines et paysages, Salon de 1767*. Paris: Hermann.

Choay, Françoise 1999: *L'allegorie du patrimoine*. Paris: Editions Seuil.

Damsholt, Tine 2000a: *Fædrelandskærlighed og borgerdyd. Patriotisk diskurs og militære reformer i Danmark i sidste del af 1700-tallet*. København: Museum Tusculanum.

Damsholt, Tine 2000b: Being moved. *Ethnologia Scandinavica*, Vol. 30, pp. 24–46.

Diderot, Denis 1767/1995: Le Salon de 1767 adressé à mon ami M. Grimm. In: Else Marie Bukdahl, Michel Delon & Annette Lorenceau (eds.), *Diderot. Ruines et paysages, Salon de 1767*. Paris: Hermann.

Eriksen, Anne 1999: *Historie, minne, myte*. Oslo: Pax forlag.

Fehrman, Carl 1956: *Ruinernas romantik. En litteraturhistorisk studie*. Stockholm: Bonniers.

Hunt, John Dixon 2004: *The Picturesque Garden in Europe*. London: Thames and Hudson.

Jensen, Bernard Eric 2003: *Historie – livsverden og fag*. København: Gyldendal.

Koselleck, Reinhart 1985: Historia magistra vitae: The dissolution of the topos into the perspective of a modernized historical process. In: *Futures Past: On the Semantics of Historical Time*. Cambridge: MIT Press.

Le Ménahèze, Sophie 2001: *l'Invention du jardin romantique en France 1761–1808*. Neuilly-sur-Seine: Editions Spiralinthe.

Macauly, Rose 1953: *Pleasure of Ruins*. London: Weidenfeld & Nicolson.

Makarius, Michel 2004: *Ruins*. Paris: Editions Flammarion.

Phillips, Mark Salber 2004: Introduction: What is tradition when it is not 'invented? In: M.S. Phillips & G. Schochet (eds.), *Questions of Tradition*. Toronto: University of Toronto Press.

Røgeberg, Kristin M. (ed.) 2003–2005: *Norge i 1743 : innberetninger som svar på 43 spørsmål fra Danske Kanselli*. Vols. 1-3. Oslo: Riksarkivet and Solum forlag.

Ruinportalen (National Heritage Board, Sweden): http://www.ruinportalen.se/ 26.11.06.

Ruinprosjektet (Directorate for Cultural Heritage, Norway): http://www.riksantikvaren.no/Norsk/Fagemner/Arkeologi/Ruiner/ 26.11.06.

Suecia antiqua et odierna: http://www.kb.se/suecia/ 26.11.06.

Sweet, Rosemary 2004: *Antiquaries. The Discovery of the Past in Eighteenth-Century Britain*. London: Hambledon and London.

Willim, Robert 2005: Återupptäckten av industrisamhället. *Rig*, No. 3, pp. 152–160.

Woodward, Christopher 2001: *In Ruins*. London: Chatto and Windus. www.english-heritage.org.uk 26.11.06.

Anne Eriksen is professor of Cultural History at the University of Oslo, Norway. Her fields of study are popular religion, collective memory and historiography. Among her recent publications are "Tradisjon og fortelling. En innføring i folkloristikk" ("Tradition and narrative. An introduction to folklore studies" With T.Selberg, 2006). Soon to appear is a study of historiography and antiquarian knowledge in Norwegian eighteenth-century topographical literature.
(anne.eriksen@ikos.uio.no)

CASTING POST-SOCIALIST MEMORY
Monuments and Memorials as Instruments of Identity Politics in the Ukraine

Viktoriya Hryaban

> Nations and communities have always preserved and disseminated symbols of their identity in order to establish and consolidate their legitimacy; the changing appearance of cities and the configuration of public space through monuments and memorials have given increased visibility to such politics. This article analyses the relationship between the aesthetics of today's Ukrainian monuments and the programmatic aims of Socialist Realism. It gives an account of the conflicts between different forms of remembering and the structural similarities in the hierarchies of those considered worthy of monuments in the Soviet Union and the independent Ukraine, thus contributing to our understanding of how national identity is marked in today's Ukraine.
>
> *Keywords:* politics of identity, Ukraine, monuments, landscape

New discourses of national identity in the successor states of the Soviet Union often seem fragmentary, conducted in an irregular, even contradictory fashion. Although they aspire to achieve coherent identities built on solid historical foundations, such discourses are doomed to failure when they meet reality in the form of political decisions, patriotic events and nationalist art. Their clear aims become clouded, and their target groups are often left perplexed in a public sphere characterised by traces of this search for identity.

An inventory of the present state of affairs in the Ukraine as regards these discourses reveals that, twelve years after the declaration of independence in 1991, the urban habitat in particular offers a promising field for investigation. The continual development and restructuring of cities make them especially suited to rendering past and present transformations visible, as they are on the one hand a privileged site of such changes, and on the other, represent them in their entirety. Among the numerous media which transmit history and identity, monuments and memorials mark central places in our cities and landscapes with their messages. Devoid of the functional value of monumental buildings, they unfold their power by their centripetal influence on the space which surrounds them and the metaphorical power of their 'material political symbolism' (Mittig 1993: 26). Observers of classic Soviet or Ukrainian statues can see the former as an unfolding of the past in a present space. Larger-than-life statues showing the human body in exaggeratedly melodramatic poses, often gesturing with raised arms, dominate the surrounding area with their representation of history and arouse in the observer a sense of the responsibility which they owe to this historical perspective. Material symbolism intensifies this effect by generalising it and making it a matter of collective responsibility. Monuments of marble, steel and bronze lay claim to consistency and collectivity, as the attributes of their materials seem to address their message not just to all contemporary observers, but also to generations to come. This is a game in which the figures on the board often fall out of favour and disappear from the public sphere as unworthy of a monument before they can really take hold of the collective memory (see Menkovic 1996). Nevertheless, each new statue of bronze, each new monument in marble is erected to last centuries. It is not surprising that the loudest calls for the use of these principles are to be found in the totalitarian systems of the early twentieth century.

In the context of National Socialist art theory, Friedrich Tamms describes the programmatic aims distilled for Nazi Germany in the 1940s in the 'law of the monumental' ('Gesetz des Monumentalen'). According to this, the monumental has to be 'useless in a practical sense, but the carrier of an idea. It has to carry something inaccessible in itself, which fills people with admiration but also with awe. It must be impersonal, because it is not the work of an individual, but the symbol of a community bound together by a common ideal' (Tamms 1944: 60). Neither the embellishment of cities nor supporting art nor honouring esteemed personages and events is central here. Instead, the monumental is driven by the active configuration of national identity and belief in the truth value of a particular history – of a national destiny.

Ill. 1: Demolition of Lenin's monument in Chernivcy, Ukraine, in 1991. (Photo by Olexander Masan.)

The Legitimisation of National Identity – History and Memory

In contrast to the established democracies of Western Europe, the question of how to deal with one's own identity crops up in almost all areas of public and private life for a young state like the Ukraine. The Declaration of Independence on 24 August 1991 drew a definitive demarcation line between 'self' and 'other' and also established clear identities and affiliations in international law. At the same time however, in other arenas, in cities, villages and communities, debates on origins, identity and their representation had only just begun. Monuments and memorials were and are a privileged form of the material representation of identity in the successor states to the Soviet Union. The dismantling and destruction of Soviet monuments in the early 1990s was primarily a matter of limiting the references to the Soviet Union which were still too omnipresent in social and political structures. The emblems and figures in stone and metal erected to replace Marx and Lenin were then used to legitimise the Ukraine as a state in the eyes of its inhabitants. Due to the Austro-Hungarian, Polish, Romanian and Soviet past of the areas which make up the Ukraine today, not to mention the Stalinist policy of enforced resettlement of whole tribes and races, the new political elite in the Ukraine saw themselves confronted with a heterogeneous population whose commitments to various ethnic, religious and linguistic groups were often contradictory.

The aim of unification under the Ukrainian trident on its yellow-blue background could therefore only be achieved by reconfiguring the symbols of identity and affiliation in all spheres of life. As Pierre Bourdieu emphasises, transformations of these symbols show the struggles between political elites over whose prerogative it is to intervene and determine or change these *lieux de memoire*, loaded as they are with historical and personal values (Bourdieu 1977,

Ill. 2: Pulling down of Lenin's monument in Hotin, Ukraine, in 1996. (Photo by Olexander Masan.)

1990; see Forest & Johnson 2001). In an attempt to preserve and extend their legitimacy and power, the political elite entered into a symbolic dialogue with their own past and with society. Above all, the erection and design of public statues and monuments represents the whole discussion process which surrounds a state's representative orientation. Groups which possess political and economic power try to prove that those persons and events which correspond to their ideas of identity and history are worthy of monuments, and to make sure that their symbols are widely disseminated. Public debate around these topoi is mostly about the past, or to be more precise, about history and the necessity of rediscovering the truth, which in this case meant eliminating Soviet propaganda and making the traces of the suppressed historiography of an independent Ukrainian nation visible once more.

In this respect, the monuments and memorials erected after 1991 are 'witnesses to a doubly historical time' (Reichel 1995: 49), as they do not only represent a particular perspective on history but also make visible the agents of this selection in the present, who through the representation of the past are trying to legitimise present and future measures. Many and disparate are the groups who engage in such practices, from politicians to societies for national heritage to the diaspora. Nevertheless, their debates on the correct way of representing Ukrainian identity share an emphasis on the history of the nation's development. However, Pierre Nora's distinction between memory and history shows that history is only ostensibly in the foreground of these debates. An understanding of history as a reconstructed representation of the past, as distinct from memory as an 'ever present phenomenon, a tie which is experienced in an eternal present' emphasises that the 'strongest of our collective traditions' (Nora 1990: 13), the configuration of our past as a collective, has less to do with honouring and handing down the past than with shaping the present and the future.

Socialist Realism and the 'Monumental Propaganda' Plan

Although formal knowledge of these functions and effects was an achievement of the late twentieth-century cultural studies movement, their strategic use to construct a collective identity had already been implemented on a grand scale in Ukrainian history at the beginning of the century by Bolshevism. The 'Monumental Propaganda' decree, signed by Lenin and published in *Pravda* on 14 April 1918 (Bowlt 1978: 185), shows how manipulation in public spaces with the help of art and architecture is aimed at forming a new identity, a new consciousness. The purpose of this decree, alongside the renaming of cities and streets, was in particular the which were to express the 'ideals and feelings of the workers of revolutionary Russia' (Izwestija 1918). On 30 July in the same year, Radnarkom (Highest Committee of the People's Commissioners) confirmed a list of 66 people, artists as well as revolutionaries, whose work was considered especially progressive and who were therefore judged to be worthy of monuments. However, to Lenin's disappointment, the removal of the 'repulsive idols, erected to the honour of the czar and his servants' did not call forth the euphoria he had hoped for. The artists commissioned expressed moderate enthusiasm. Only after several invitations had been issued were 30 provisional monuments of plaster, cement and wood erected to mark the first anniversary of the revolution in Moscow. After a 'people's debate', 17 of them were to be conferred the honour of lasting preservation in bronze and stone. This plan was never carried out in full, as both the political leaders and the people were dissatisfied with the results. The art historian N. Radlow attributed the failure of this monumental plan, not to the sculptors' lack of ability, but to the 'conditions of the time: life was lived by the day and did not encourage in any way the execution of monumental tasks, which require calm synthesis' (Radlow 1923: 35). This assessment by a contemporary figure illustrates clearly what seems to be a prerequisite for developing the power of monuments as the projection surface of a future which has been ennobled by monumental promises.

In Kiev, the capital of the Ukraine, the realisation of this plan began on 7 May 1919. One of the first monuments to be removed in 1917 was the statue of P. Stolpyn, chairman of the council of ministers under Nicolai II. By 1923, 8 further monuments had been dismantled, including statues of Czars Nicolai I and Alexander III. Amongst the monuments that had been newly erected, there was a statue of the Ukrainian poet Taras Schewtschenko (1814–1861), to whose functional value as a symbol and figurehead for both the Soviet Union and the Ukraine will be discussed later in this article.

The 'Monumental Propaganda' plan clearly shows how in Leninist theory the artist as political agitator was rework his material, to shape the urban environment according to socialist ideals. However, although its function and content were predetermined, no-one could agree on how this art should look. The debates on stylistic alignment took place at the beginning of the 1920s in a climate of increasing politicisation of art and representation, as they were incorporated more and more in the regime's apparatus. As part of this process, art was given the didactic task of translating the politics and ideology of communism in a language which everyone could understand. At the end of the 1920s and in the early 1930s, the production of art, in large quantities and organised in production centres, was already an established part of the state information machine. The main 'buyer', if not the only one, was the state. Soon the range of memorials was extended to include all the shining lights of the communist view of history. Busts and monuments of philosophers, writers, artists and academics, typically, realistically and geo-

Ill. 3: Lenin monuments erected in the Soviet Union. (Above from the left: Chernivtsy, Kiev (UA), Ulan Ude (RU), down from the left: Pryluky (UA), Grutas (LT), Sankt-Petersburg (RU), Kiev (UA).

metrically correct, found their way into the smallest and most remote communities. After 1932, artistic production finally fixed on the term 'Socialist Realism'. At this time, the whole country was already flooded with strictly uniform statues and monuments, from the large, sometimes huge images of Marx and Lenin in cities, flanked by the 'big buildings of communism' right down to more modest depictions of workers and sportsmen and women in public parks.

It would be wrong to conclude however that this uniform aesthetic, always produced in the same combinations as if on a conveyor belt, was ideologically driven mimesis. Boris Groys describes the mimetic character of Socialist Realist painting as 'just an illusion (...) just one of very many ideologically motivated messages' (Groys 1996: 63). Instead, Socialist Realism defined itself through its methods. Firstly, the artist had to choose the right contents and symbols to represent and order the ideals of real socialism, and secondly, these ideals had to be transmitted in a form which would be comprehensible to the working population. The term 'realism' can quickly become misleading here, as it conceals the fact that it was not a matter of mimetically portraying reality, but projecting the blessing of a communist future, making it visible (Groys 1996: 142). In this way, works of art such as monuments were meant to symbolise the collective and individual dream of a new world and a new identity. The task of Socialist Realism lay in showing life in its revolutionary development: national in its form and socialist in its content (Groys 1994: 16).

These two worlds were already difficult enough to get to harmonise with each other, but it seemed practically impossible for the artists executing the monuments to remain faithful to the contradictory directives of the party leadership. When analysing Socialist Realism, it is therefore also important to consider the working conditions under which it was produced. The atmosphere of the time is shown clearly in an article by the architect Karo Alabjan published in 1936, 'Against Formalism, Schematism and Eclecticism' (Alabjan 1936). No art history background is needed here to see that very little space was left for professions of expressive freedom. In accordance with Stalin, Alabjan formulated the paradoxical rule which decreed that every single form of architecture and art was to be subjected to merciless criticism. Both clear and simple forms as well as contradictory and experimental designs were considered treacherous. The prevailing suspicion, one which proved fatal for some artists, was that stylistic purity and adherence to principles of form were only possible for a bourgeois consciousness. Communist artists were confronted with the demand to unify contradictory elements. The 'superhuman monumental' had simultaneously to create an 'intimate, human and cosy' effect (Groys 1994: 17). The people's greatness had to be emphasised as much as the life of the individual worker. The theory behind this is taken from the dialectics of historical materialism, according to which only the sum of the contradictions and paradoxes of all the individual art works together can establish their inner similarities and therefore the idea of Soviet society. However, in the final instance, Alabjan's article does not contain a concrete answer to the question which remains the main issue to this day: how a statue should look, how and where it should be erected, and how it should embody its target ideals.

N. A. Bulganin and L. Kaganovitsch, both Stalinist spokesmen, specified a possible answer to this question at the congress of Soviet architects in 1937 with a call for 'highly qualified creation' (Bulganin 1937: 18). High quality production was to ensure that the absolute was represented in all individual work in an ideal form. The charisma of several individual works was to provide an ensemble which in turn would represent a city, a country and eventually, the nation. A hint as to what was to be depicted in such a 'highly qualified' way can be found in the writings of G. M. Malenkov, member of the Politbureau and Stalin's private secretary. Art and architecture should represent 'the typical'. According to Malenkov, 'Our artists, writers and performers must always show awareness in their work that the typical is not that which is most common, but that which expresses the essence of a particular social force with the greatest persuasive power' (Report from the 19th Party Conference. Quoted by Groys 1996: 58). When we look at the aesthetics of Soviet monuments, it becomes clear that this 'essence' was thought to be in the expressive power of lofty gestures and larger-than-life statues and tableaux.

Transformations of Memory in Today's Ukraine

When we compare this Soviet symbolic ideal with the aesthetics of the anthropocentric statues and monuments which have been erected in the Ukraine since 1991, it becomes clear that the planning of memorials and cities with protagonists of a collective Ukrainian identity follows an almost identical pathos of immediacy and candour. The obvious conclusion would seem to be that typically Ukrainian content is being propagated using the patterns of the discarded Soviet tradition. Shortly after the collapse of the Soviet Union the new (old) Ukrainian elites began to spread propaganda for the idea of a new Ukrainian identity through statues and monuments, using the symbolism of Socialist Realism that had been established for decades. Like chess pieces on a board which is centuries old, figures were changed on the pedestals where previously czarist and Soviet representatives had embodied the unity and absolutism of their respective systems.

The monuments to B. Chmelnyzky, a Ukrainian Hetman (Cossak ruler), and M. Zanjkowezka, a Ukrainian actress, were presented to the public in 1993 on the 1000th anniversary of the foundation of the city of Nizyn in the Tschernihiv region. In Dnepropetrowsk, a memorial was erected to D. Javornyzky, a member of the Academy of Sciences. Statues followed of Kiril and Mephodij, the inventors of the Cyrillic alphabet, also of Princess Olga, unveiled 1996 in Kiev, of J. Fedkowitsch in 1995 in Chernivci, and of K. Haiskoij, builder of a steel works in Luchansk, in 1996. After the unveiling of a monuments to the arts patron J. Charitonenko in Summy 1996, memorials to Prince Jaroslav Mudryj were unveiled in Kiev 1997 and in Charkiv in 1999, to Prince Roman Mstyslavitsch in Kolky in 1997, to the academic, folklorist and teacher O. Duchnovitsch in Uzgorod in 1997, in Kiev to the first president of the Ukraine Hruschewsky, in 1998 and in Chernivci to the singer Nazar Jaremtschuk in December 1998 (Lytvyn 2000: 153ff).

This list could be continued ad infinitum. The common denominator shared by all these erections and inaugurations is the absolute commitment to an archaeology of the Ukraine's own identity in the places where history had been staged by the 'other' before 1991. This process of course demands a dynamic of distancing or disassociation from the Soviet past, however when looked at closer, this dynamic is counteracted by the use of aesthetic means which are taken from this very same tradition.

Lenin's successor on the main squares of the bigger cities and on the walls of public spaces was the 'Father of the Ukrainian Nation', Taras Schewtschenko. Readings and ceremonies in Schewtschenko's honour have been held since the declaration of independence in all Ukrainian towns and villages. Innumerable statues have been dedicated to him, to name just a selected few: in 1992 in Chernihiv, 1995 in Luzk, 1998 in Luchansk and in 1999 in Uzgorod and Chernivci. In 1994, the 180th anniversary of Schewtschenko's birthday, ceremonial inspections of the monuments dedicated to him were carried out in Charkiv, Tscherkasy and Lviv (Lytvyn 2000: 65ff; *Zberezhemo...* 2003: 2).

Post-1991 Ukraine was not the first to recognise Schewtschenko's suitability as a marker of the transition from a history determined by others to self-determined history. His biography had already been redefined as that of a revolutionary hero under the Soviets. For the Bolshevists, Schewtschenko was a prime example of imperial oppression by the czarist regime. The monument 'Kobsar' to the former serf and poet was erected in Kiev in 1918, and was supposed to show the Ukrainians the difference between czarist oppression and the Soviets' tolerance of national distinctions (Wanner 1998: 177). Whilst Schewtschenko was never at the top of the Soviet hierarchy and therefore never to be found on main squares in cities, he has now been given the leading role as far as the staging of Ukrainian tradition and history are concerned. The repression of the Russian monarchy is no longer considered to have been directed at the protester and revolutionary who demanded social equality, but at the nationalist Ukrainian democrat and artist. Schewtschenko has proved himself to be a national figure of identification, a carefully chosen middle way in contrast to the radical nationalists and former fighters for the Ukrainian cause such as Stepan Bandera (Head of the Organization of Ukrainian Nationalists). These contradictory uses of a historical figure show very clearly how the meaning and function of a sign can be transformed according to its location within a network of contextual reference.

The concerted iconoclasm which had to precede these changes was not however equally successful throughout the country. Along the historic borders from before 1944, an East–West divide has also become clear in monument politics. Whilst Lenin can still be seen in more than one Eastern city, larger-than-life and pointing to the Soviet legacy with his lifted arm, the Lenin statue on the main square of Lviv, the cultural centre of the West Ukraine, was destroyed with a crane as early as 1990 by an enthusiastic, cheering crowd. A hole was left which slowly filled with water, and a fountain recalled the mighty fallen until a statue of Schewtschenko was erected shortly after as a replacement. In Kiev the Lenin statue on the former Square of the October Revolution was daubed in August 1991 with swastikas and the words 'Satan' and 'Fuck'. The original plan was to demolish the statue by explosion, but as it had been erected over a metro station, this idea was discarded, and it was then dismantled piece by piece. Today this place is overloaded with advertisements for foreign banks, computer firms and soft drinks manufacturers. Lenin, the icon of Socialism, has been replaced by new signs of capitalist hegemony in the service of stimulating consumerism. It seems easier to dispose of and forget representations of Soviet ideology in this way than by using the protagonists of a Ukrainian identity (Wanner 1998: 183–185).

The question of how to treat the monuments of obsolete empires and systems remains controversial today, as does that of the necessity and justification for new statues. Contemporary Ukraine has developed varying strategies for dealing with these legacies, ranging from demands for the removal of all representations which do not fit in the framework of nationalist Ukrainian identity concepts, to the practice of leaving the old symbols in their place as relics which have been devalued by the progress of history. In Charkiv, in the Eastern Ukraine, the latter strategy was chosen, and the bulky, 20 meters high Lenin statue erected in 1963 was left on the Square of Independence, the second largest square in the world after Tiananmen Square. It is no surprise that this square then became a favourite location for protests and opposition marches.

Conflicts between two different concepts of collective remembrance also arose during the planning and erection of a Schewtschenko memorial in Luchansk. As early as 1992, the city council decided to place a Schewtschenko statue on the city's main square. However, it was unable to provide the funds for such an expensive project. Eventually, at the instigation of the organisation 'Supporters of Schewtschenko' founded in 1995, a world-wide fund-raising drive began. The sculptor Ivan Chumak emerged victoriously from a competition also held in 1995 with the plan for a 5½ meters high bronze statue of Schewtschenko with a granite pedestal. The funding available within the Ukraine, 30,000 hrivna from the city council, 10,000 hrivna from the government and 20,000 hrivna from private sponsors, was nowhere near enough to finance the project. Only after an appeal had been launched to the Ukrainian diaspora, above all in Canada and the USA, was it possible to begin building with a further $50,000 of donations. It then transpired that the site originally intended was not viable for geological reasons, and so it was decided that the monument be erected in the place which until then had been named for the fallen of the Second World War and dedicated to their memory. Fierce protests against the name change and the erection of the new statue broke out amongst veterans' associations, supported by left-wing political factions. Appeals from the 'Supporters of Schewtschenko' to President Kutschma and threats from the war veterans were the despair of the newly elected mayor Jevremov, who was caught between the two fronts. The struggle between these two cults of the dead finally concluded, to the veterans' satisfaction, with the erection of an additional memorial in honour of the fallen of the Second World War, and, to the satisfaction of the supporters of the Ukrainian nationalist cause, with the erection of the Schewtschenko monument without its granite pedestal in the place it was originally planned for. This shows what an important role the commemoration of the dead of the Second World War still plays in society today as far as the identity formation of survivors is concerned. It also shows how easy it is for this to collide with other forms of remembrance.

Institutionalised Forms of Representation

Victory over National Socialism and Fascism was one of the formative experiences of the former Soviet Union. It marked a turning point in the history of the USSR, a shift in international geo-politics which in turn caused fundamental changes in the situation within the Soviet Union. Memorials grew in size and pathos; Western fear of the Soviet Union's military might was stylised and the heroism of its population was immortalised throughout the land in enormous complexes and monuments. Whilst in the big cities whole landscapes were created anew for this purpose, people limited themselves to the erection of less expensive symbols in smaller towns. Although these representations exploited the violent death of millions to legitimise the actions of former and present rulers and to make 'the private character of mourning a matter of national concern' (Menkovic 1996) in the former Soviet Union, these monuments have survived the transition to Ukrainian independence astonishingly well.

The most impressive reminder of this tradition is the 'Batkivshchina' in Kiev, which dominates the cityscape with its surrounding set of reliefs, statues, tanks, aeroplanes and anti-aircraft guns from the Second World War. Today this place is used by the population above all for recreation, as a destination for excursions and a popular place for representative photographs after ceremonies, birthdays and weddings. In smaller towns, this commemorative practice is recalled by monuments to the first soldiers to liberate the place, tanks on pedestals which were the first to break through enemy lines, a gravestone with the names of the dead or a red star. Even after Ukrainian independence, representations of collective experiences of suffering and catastrophe are a privileged theme for monumental representations in the public sphere. The forms of representation of Ukrainian identity and history chosen by decision-makers in these cases can help us trace development of visual interventions in urban space with reference to what being Ukrainian is supposed to mean.

A classic monument to the victims of the Second World War was completed in Kovel, in the Wolyn region, in 1996. In Wolyn itself, a memorial was erected in 1995 to the Ukrainian soldiers who fell in Afghanistan, and in Chernivci for the soldiers of Kuryn in the Bukowina.[1] Further monuments were unveiled in Poltawa in 1999 to the fallen Ukrainian Cossaks, in Rubiznyj[2] and in Chernivci in 1999 for the soldiers who died in Afghanistan between 1979 and 1989. In Ivano-Frankivsk the bell tower was publicly dedicated to the memory of the victims of Bolshevik terror in 1998. Not just war and terror are to be remembered: a monument put up in Chernivci in 2002 commemorates the helpers who died as a result of the reactor accident in Chernobyl (Lytvyn 2000: 286ff; *Zberezhemo...* 2003: 3).

The structures of standardised representative ideals to be seen in these monuments are nothing new when considered against a background of traditional Soviet town planning. Memorials and monuments have been given an important and clearly regulated place in the configuration of urban space, according to their subject matter and how they present it. In analogy to the hierarchies of the Soviet Union, the politics of representation and the construction of a Ukrainian identity through monuments also have a clearly defined structure. This legacy applies to a wide range of monuments, from the replacement of Lenin by Schewtschenko, to the adoption of the memorials to the many wars, right up to the artists and writers. The statues of Schiller and Goethe from the early 20th century were replaced by Marx and Robespierre, and today have been replaced yet again by statues of the Ukrainian poet Lesja Ukrainka and the Ukrainian philosopher Ivan Franko. There are

Ill. 4: Monuments erected in the Ukraine since the independence in commemoration of tragic pages of Ukrainian history: Wars, Great Famine (1932–1933), Chernobyl catastrophe.

however also considerable differences between the Soviet Union and today's Ukraine, not least of which is the discrepancy in the means at their disposal. More important still are the different purposes of their respective identity politics. Soviet intervention aimed to embody the idea of a nation 'outside the limits of history', the supposed conclusion of socio-political evolution in an eschatological final stage of scientific socialism, whereas the Ukraine is endeavouring to create a fully valid democratic state modelled on Western European lines.

The representative forms of the new Ukrainian statues conform in almost every case to the Socialist Realist models from the time of Stalin. In opposition to Kant's definition of art as 'disinterested pleasure', the politics of landscaping still follow the Leninist idea of using the suggestive and regulating power of art in the public sphere to construct and consolidate a sphere of self-identity.

Even if these new monuments harmonise with the existing urban panorama, this cannot conceal the fact that they are ultimately the means for partitioning, domesticating and marking cities as sites of ideological struggle. The power of images and embodiments represents the symbolic instance of law and demands loyalty from those who behold them. Through their strategic position in big squares, their functions change quicker than their planners would like. Rituals such as mass demonstrations and protests do not care about the aims of those who erected the monuments, but use the power of these *lieux de memoire* for their own purposes.

The changes which take place are generally quickly integrated into people's daily lives. In the first days and weeks, monuments are enthusiastically received or rejected, soon however they become barely noticeable. Robert Musil's dictum that 'there is nothing in the world as invisible as a monument' (Musil 1936: 87), opens up a further debate as to whether contemporary aesthetics, not to mention the representative forms of monuments and memorials per se, can still function as a modern way of remembering at all.

Nonetheless, the cases described above depict the transition in the politics of memory from the Russian monarchy to the Soviet Union and on to the successor 'New Independent States', and open up possibilities for observing the shifting configurations of hierarchies, classifications and categories. The specific visibility of these processes in the Ukraine are therefore not only markers of current changes in the representation of national identity, but can also be used to uncover the underlying vocabulary of symbolic deformation, change and replacement which are at work whenever and wherever monuments are erected.

Notes
1. Part of the armed Ukrainian Resistance.
2. To be found in Rubiznyj in the classic representative form of a tank in attack mode on a pedestal.

References

Alabjan, Karo 1936: Protiv formalisma, uproschchenija i eklektiki. *Architektura USSR*, No. 4., pp. 1–5.

Bourdieu, Pierre 1977: *Outline of a Theory of Practice*. Cambrige: Cambridge University Press.

Bourdieu, Pierre 1990: *The Logic of Practice*. Stanford: Stanford University Press.

Bowlt, John E. 1978: Russian Sculpture and Lenin's plan of Monumental Propaganda. In: Henry A. Millon & Linda Nochlin (eds.), *Art and Architecture in the Service of Politics*. Cambrige, Mass.: MIT Press, pp. 182–193.

Bulganin, Nikolaj 1937: Rekonstructsija gorodov, schilishchnoe stroitelstvo i zadachi architekturi. *Architektura USSR*, Moskva. No. 7–8.

Drengenberg, Hans 1972: *Die sowjetische Politik auf dem Gebiet der bildenden Kunst von 1917 bis 1934*. Berlin: Ost-Europa-Institut an der Freien Universität Berlin, Historische Veröffentlichungen, Bd. 16.

Forest, Benjamin & Juliet Johnson 2001: *Unraveling the Thread of History: Soviet-Era National Identity in Moskow*. Revised for the Annals of the Association of American Geographers. August 2001:4.

Gaßner, Hubertus 1993: Sowjetische Denkmäler im Aufbau. In: Michael Diers (ed.), *Mo(nu)mente: Formen und Funktionen ephemerer Denkmäler*. Berlin: Akademischer Verlag, pp. 153–178.

Groys, Boris 1994: Die gebaute Ideologie. In: Peter Noever (ed.), *Tyrannei des Schönen: Architektur der Stalin-Zeit*. München, New York: Prestel, pp. 15–21.

Groys, Boris 1996: *Gesamtkunstwerk Stalin. Die gespaltene Kultur in der Sowjetunion*. München, Wien: Carl Hanser Verlag.

Iswestija 1918. 14 April. Moscow.

Lytvyn, V. M. 2000: *Ukraina: Chronika postupu (1991–2000)*. Kiev: Vidavnychyj dim "Alternatyvy".

Menkovic, Boljana 1996: Politische Gedenkkultur: Die Visualisierung politischer Macht im öffentlichen Raum. Diplomarbeit an der Universität Wien.

Mittig, Hans-Ernst 1993: Dauerhaftigkeit, einst Denkmalargument. In: Michael Diers (ed.), *Mo(nu)mente: Formen und Funktionen ephemerer Denkmäler*. Berlin: Akademie Verlag, pp. 11–34.

Musil, Robert 1936: *Nachlaß zu Lebzeiten*. Zürich: Humanitas.

Nora, Pierre 1990: *Zwischen Geschichte und Gedächtnis*. Berlin: Verlag Klaus Wagenbach.

Radlow, Nikolaj. 1923: Die Russische Kunst von 1917–1922. In: *Das heutige Russland 1917–1922, Wirtschaft und Kultur in der Darstellung Russischer Forscher*, Berlin 1923. Quotation after Gaßner 1993.

Reichel, Peter 1995: *Politik mit der Erinnerung*. München, Wien: Carl Hanser Verlag.

Tamms, Friedrich 1944: Das Grosse in der Baukunst. In: *DKiDR Die Baukunst*. Hg. von Beauftragten des Führers für die gesamte geistige und weltanschauliche Erziehung der NSDAP. Januar, 47–60.

Wanner, Catherine 1998: *Burden of Dreams: History and Identity in Post-Soviet Ukraine*. Pennsylvania: The Pennsylvania State University Press.

Zberezhemo dla naschchadkiv pamjat, vtilenu u kameni i metali (Pamjatnyky mista Chernivci, sporudzheni protjagom 1992–2002). 2003. Chernivtci.

Viktoriya Hryaban, PhD, finished her research in Bukowina for the project "Center/Periphery in the Rule and Culture of the Habsburg Monarchy 1867–1918" at the Vienna University in January 2006. She is currently working with a project on the Europeanization in the Ukraine.
(hryaban@gmx.net)

TURKISH LACE
Constructing Modernities and Authenticities

Hilje van der Horst

> Turkish domesticity is often associated with lace doilies. While this decoration practice is diminishing, it can still be encountered in a large number of Turkish Dutch houses in the Netherlands. However, Turkish lace appears in a variety of other settings in the Netherlands as well, such as shops and exhibition spaces. In these diverse settings a wide variety of actors give it meaning. While notions of modernity, tradition and authenticity are present in all settings, they are understood in conflicting ways. Non-Turkish actors, handling this lace, co-define it, as well as a broader concept of Turkishness.
>
> *Keywords:* Turkish migrants, lace, material culture, authenticity, modernity

Any person who has visited the houses of Turkish migrants or their descendants in the Netherlands, has probably encountered lace doilies[1] in at least some of them. Typically, lace doilies hang over the front of shelves in glass cabinets, cover coffee tables and very often also cover the upper part of televisions, refrigerators and ovens. Turks are by no means unique in this. The Netherlands itself has had a tradition of lace making and decorating (see Stone-Ferrier 1991). Lace has many old-fashioned, even archaic associations, but I want to show in opposition to those associations that it is a rich vehicle for studying the dynamic nature of material culture. Lace is relevant to the construction of Turkish identities. Turks, or descendants of migrated Turks, however, are not the only ones who possess this 'Turkish' lace and give it meanings. As will become clear in the course of this article, lace that bears Turkish associations figures in many settings and has a complex geography.

By looking at lace in a variety of contexts, I aim to gain an understanding of the different processes of meaning production that surround it and the variety of actors involved. The contexts through which lace moves belong both to the public and to the private sphere. In these different contexts I look at how lace often carries conflicting connotations, how an aura of authenticity is installed, and how this intersects with connotations of modernity. Firstly, the practice of lace making in Turkish families will be addressed. Secondly, the different commercial settings in which lace with a Turkish connotation is traded will come to the fore. Then, thirdly, the paper will deal with two organizations that are professionally involved in the lace making practice. Lastly, the different projects in which the lace making practice is brought into the public arena and festivalised will be addressed.

Contesting a Cultural Practice in the Turkish Dutch Family

At the beginning of my fieldwork, I conducted an interview with a Turkish woman, called Özlem,[2] and her daughter Hülya.[3] I contacted Özlem because she was on a list of participants in a Turkish amateur art festival and had entered a piece of needlework in the contest. She told me that she also participated in a Turkish women's group in a local community centre, in which they made needlework and knitted together. After being shown some of her products, such as a knitted scarf and a richly-decorated hand towel for the kitchen, I asked her about the lace doily that was on the coffee table and was covered by a glass plate. She told me that she did not make this doily herself. In fact, none of the doilies on display in her house, in the glass cases, in the cupboard and on the small round table in a corner of the room, were her own creation. All had been bought in shops. The objects she made herself were made more for fun and social interaction than anything else.

'Do you not have a bridal chest filled with homemade textiles?' I asked. I had previously been told by several people that many Turkish women, especially from the countryside, start working on their trousseau, with needlework and other kinds of textile decoration, something which is called a *çeyiz* in Turkish, early on or preferably even before their teens. Many of them, especially in the past, as was the case with my informant, stopped with their education after elementary school and filled a portion of their days with this very laborious task from that moment onwards. It was expected of a good girl, I was told, that she occupy herself with this task, and in the process prepared herself for marriage.[4]

This practice fits in a specific gender ideology and is effective in keeping women who pass from being girls to becoming women inside the house, where they occupy themselves with 'female' activities rather than children's play. The objects in the chest were said to be used during the rest of a woman's life to decorate her house and, possibly during economic hardship, women could even sell pieces to supplement the family income. Just as in Bourdieu's analysis of the Kabyle house (1979), the practice is the product of and reflects a certain gender ideology and is effective in naturalizing and reproducing this ideology.

Özlem, in fact, did have a bridal chest, which she had filled while growing up in Turkey. However, the things in it were not fashionable anymore, she told me. Therefore she preferred to buy things from the shops. According to her, the doily on her coffee table was the latest fashion in Turkish households in the Netherlands. Many of her friends had a similar piece. It struck me only after the interview that she did not even show me the objects of her trousseau, even though she fetched everything else the instant that I showed any interest in them, or had her daughter fetch them. This was not something she was very proud of, although she did cherish it. Although the practice of decorating the house with needlework is sometimes interpreted as part of tradition, it has in fact changed immensely. Doilies may be used to claim a modern identity, in combination with Turkishness, much like some forms of the Sari have become means to combine an Indian with a modern identity (Banerjee & Miller 2003).

Interesting were also the comments of the daughter, who was in the first year of a school for intermediate vocational education, learning to become an interior designer. She made it clear to me that she was not planning on creating and assembling her own trousseau as she wanted to 'do everything modern', which, in her understanding of it, was in opposition to everything Turkish.

Ill. 1: Store bought doilies in a Turkish Dutch interior. (Photo by the author.)

– In the past she used to start 'buy that, maybe you will use it in the future'. I do not want such things in my house. That is, for example, the bridal chest, that you still have. Like pans and cutlery and everything. We just do not want that. My mother tells me, 'buy it buy it, then you already have it ready'. We just don't want that.

– But you and your sister, or ...

– Me and my sister want everything modern. Really like a totally different style from the Turkish style.

– So these doilies you would never ...

– No totally not, I now do interior design as an education so I have totally changed my choice.

– But isn't there something that you do still like, or do you want everything totally different?

– If I would [consider] it modern. I would want a bridal chest, like old ones that you have, I would want to use that as table, but for the rest totally nothing. Just that as the only thing, but next to that...I find this just really typically Turkish, I wanted to say. Because if I go to friends I just see exactly the same. Then I already do not like it anymore. Then I say to my mother, 'shall we change it?'

Interestingly, this girl saw the antique bridal chest, used as a coffee table, as something modern, but not the new lace doilies that her mother bought in shops. Such chests are infrequent in the houses of Turkish families in the Netherlands, as many *çeyizler* in the Netherlands are stored in plastic bags, cupboards or boxes, whereas lace doilies are plentiful. Possibly also due to the now fashionable colonial style, in which old wooden chests frequently occur, this girl can regard the antique chest as modern.

Özlem told me that the younger generation had no interest in *çeyizler*, a statement that was confirmed by her daughter and in other interviews. Hülya was not going to do any needlework or knitting, even though she appreciated the long scarf her mother knitted for her. The only way in which a bridal chest would enter her house, was as a coffee table, not as a storage place for decorated textiles. But Özlem had also changed her attitude towards needlework. It was a hobby that she performed at a community centre, in the company of other Turkish women. She did not, however, feel that she had to prove her qualities as a housewife by filling her house with hand-made objects. Rather, she aspired to a modern image, at least within the Turkish community. Following the fashions of her group of reference was one of the tactics she followed. The daughters, like their mother, aspired to a modern image, but their points of reference were not defined by people of Turkish descent, but by school, the Dutch media and music, to name but a few. Their tight, fashionable clothes, showing their midriff, were coherent with this. The mother accepted her daughter's strive for modernity, even though it took a different shape from her own.

The generational change with regard to the making of needlework is not limited to migrants and their children. Many girls who grow up in Turkey, especially in more urban, educated and wealthy surroundings, also find the practice old-fashioned. A girl I interviewed, who recently came to the Netherlands in order to train to become a doctor, burst out in laughter when I brought up the subject of lace making, much like I would respond if someone would seriously question me about the wearing and making of wooden shoes. To her it belonged to another world; a world to which she did not belong. She stressed the fact that she respects the girls who stayed at home to do their needlework while she was pursuing her education. This can be interpreted as an attempt to compensate for the fact that she, in fact, disqualified them as rather 'backward'.

With subsequent interviews, the contested nature of this practice became even more prominent. Though some obviously turn their back on it, other women still engage, in one way or another, with the practice, although they give it various meanings. Some of the women I spoke to mentioned that they did needlework and other textile crafts because it relaxed their minds. Other women liked the needlework because to them it represented something of their Turkish past and connected them to this past. One woman put it nicely as she explained that it is the story around the çeyiz that attracts her. This woman did not want to have a glass cabinet with lace, nor lace on her television, tables and cupboards. As a young girl, however, she had a romantic image of marriage. The çeyiz making triggered her fantasies of being a princess-like bride in the future. In addition, it was one of the practices she connected with adulthood. In 'playing to be an adult' she once took her needlework with her when she visited a friend, as she saw her mother do when she made visits. During the visit she felt proud that she could show her friend her newly-acquired skill. This sensation soon disappeared when she showed her mother her progress. The mother laughed at the sight of the badly-made piece. That was the end of çeyiz making for this woman.

Even though she did not make needlework, this woman felt she belonged to the story around it. Her mother made a çeyiz for her wedding even though she always said she would never use it. After her marriage she took some of the pieces that she particularly liked and some that were practical, but left the rest with her mother. She told me that when she would have a daughter, this daughter would have something like a çeyiz. She did not expect her future daughters to use it, but this was a way for her to include them in one of the stories, not only about her own family and upbringing, but also a story that, in her mind, connected people from Turkish descent, which was particularly important to her as she married a Dutch man. They were important life story objects (Lene & Pederson, 1998), to her.

The çeyiz practice proved to be a topic that many people thought about, as it dealt with deeper issues, such as modernity and Turkishness. It also illustrates the varied meanings given to cultural practices. As Cohen (1985) argues, many practices that are used as symbolic markers are contested and have a multitude of meanings projected onto them.

Even though there is diversity in the valorisation of needlework, there still seems to be one central meaning that is widely accepted. The practice is dominantly evaluated as something constituting a 'Turkish identity'. The designs of the needlework show many regional varieties (see also Onuk 1981), giving women ample opportunities to focus on those differences as a vehicle to stress a regional background. However, this is not what they are doing. They consider it as something shared throughout the Turkish state territory. The varieties are seen as inherent in the richness of Turkish culture rather than as a threat to national unity, which is a very common aspect of Turkish nationalism.

The meanings people give to the lace are intertwined with their material practices. Through them they also position themselves vis-à-vis the making and using of lace and the group that associates itself with this lace. In some cases women decide to keep all doilies out of their house. As they are aware of the custom, this can be seen as a way of positioning themselves against the people they associate with it. One woman I visited is interesting in this respect. Although she does have two glass cabinets, a place where many Turkish women would put their doilies, her objects stand directly on the glass. She expresses a strong dislike for this practice, with which she is very familiar. Seen within her social context, even though she can decide not to engage in the practice, she cannot easily escape positioning herself against it (see also Katschnig-Fasch 1998).

Women who are critical of the practice sometimes tie it to certain gender expectations that they are confronted with. In several cases, women pointed out that they actually felt held down by the doilies. As they had to be cleaned and ironed regularly this consumed a lot of time, time that you could spend in many other ways. But it is not just the using up of time that they object to; it is that of time spent in the role of a particular kind of housewife. The doilies forced them into a performance that they are unhappy with. It is, to a large extent, this performativity that constitutes certain gender identities (see also Butler 1990). Interestingly, the material objects themselves add agency to the performance. In two cases, daughters removed the doilies in their mother's house because they did not want their mother to be cleaning them all the time. Two women replaced the doilies with plastic coasters. These coasters could be cleaned easily, but, on the other hand, were consistent with the idea that decorative objects have to stand on something and with a notion of female 'care for the home'.

Commodifying Turkish Lace

Whereas various historians, anthropologists and ethnologists have given us very nuanced descriptions of the varieties of shopping experiences and settings (see for example Miller 1994, 1998), much of the recent work that has been done in consumption studies, pays little attention to the variety of practices that fall under this general header of 'consumption'. At the same time, a division is made between 'good' shopping and 'bad' shopping. The good, to take the example of Zukin's recent book (2004), is small-scale, organic and of superior quality and is sold by true craftsmen who know about their product and are proud to share it with you. The bad is personified in Gap, Dolce & Gabbana and Banana Republic, or, in a European context, Hennes & Mauritz, Ikea and Mexx, characterized by its large-scale, bored employees and overall lack of 'authenticity'. There may be some merits in this evaluation, and I do not wish to dispute it now. What I do regret, though, is that this moral division is so powerful that it blurs a view on the immense diversity in shopping experiences and how it interacts with other cultural practices. Miller (1998) deconstructs this moral division and shows how big brands such as Heinz' soup or Kellogg's cereal can become the objectification of family tradition and love between family members. Through consumption, such objects become personified, and develop into the expression of our intricate social relations. In this section, a wide variety of settings in which 'Turkish' lace is commodified, is reviewed. Although they are positioned on both sides of the aforementioned moral division, strikingly similar processes take place.

The first keeps us within the houses of Turkish families. During my visit to Özlem's family, a neighbour came into the house, inviting all women to come to the house three doors down the road. As she explained, a woman was selling headscarves with a handmade border of needlework there (*oya* in Turkish). As I had expressed my interest in handmade objects, I was taken along. Everybody kissed each other at least three times on the cheeks and the women did not make an exception for me. After we sat down, one older woman, the one who was selling the scarves, picked up her needle and thread and continued with the piece she was working on.

On the coffee table was a plastic bag with a pile of about ten neatly folded cotton headscarves, each with a needlework border. They sold at ten euros apiece, which seems to be a small amount considering that it took the woman three days[5] to make one. The woman, described as *kapalli*, or 'closed',[6] by Hülya, was not allowed to work outside. This was one of the acceptable ways for her to add to the family income. The selling of headscarves in this fashion was not only guided by economic motives, but also gave an arena for the stressing of cultural values involved in the practice.

The women discussed the colour schemes of the scarves. One woman told me that a reason for making the border oneself is that the colours can be picked and combined better. Similar bordered scarves are also for sale in shops, but, according to her, the colours of these often do not match. Also, she explained, the patterns often change and inventors of new patterns often try to keep the instructions for making them to themselves. These innovations are simultaneously sign, consequence and cause of the fact that it is a practice that is considered alive and not to be relegated to the realm of history or forgotten traditions. Even though the women there also realized that it was not as widely practiced anymore in the Netherlands and also diminishing in importance in Turkey, they still adhered to the virtue and importance of the practice. By means of this selling, they were able to express their prolonged adherence to the practice and the idea that Turkish women should engage in it. The two daughters were addressed in this respect. Somebody said half serious, half laughingly that they had to start doing their needlework as well, as they were reaching their marriageable age. One of them smartly replied that they were an exception and did not have to do this.

For Özlem, the practice forms part of her spare time. It is a hobby and she would not dream of making it into a trade. With her cleaning job she can earn much more than one could ever earn by selling headscarves, whereas selling, and thus commodification, was part of the reality of lace making for the family in which the scarves were sold. The tradition and the commodification are intertwined. Commodification even served as a vehicle for emphasizing the values that support the practice.

An almost diagonally different setting in which Turkish lace is commodified can be found in the wholesale company called the *Woonkaravaan*, or 'living caravan'. Plastic fake lace, sold on rolls, is the best-selling item of this company, which is specialized in imported goods from Turkey. The plastic lace is sold to trendy home decorating boutiques throughout the Netherlands. Alpay, with whom I held an interview in February 2004, has a Turkish father and a Dutch mother and is the founder of this wholesale company. She travels to Turkey once every six to eight weeks, visiting shops, workplaces and factories throughout the country, on the lookout for products that are both 'oriental' and modern. She does not search for objects that would, in her words, fit into a 'thousand and one nights' fantasy interior – the interior imagined to have been present in the harems and other rich places of the Ottoman Empire. Rather, she looks for things that can fit in a Dutch trendy middle-class home: things that can be matched with designer furniture and light modern spaces. On the other hand, the Woonkaravaan uses the exotic or oriental feeling that certain products from Turkey entice in Dutch middle class consumers. It is this that, according to Alpay, attracts them to buy.

Plastic lace imported from Turkey is put to different purposes in the showroom of the Woonkaravaan. On the table at which we sat during the interview there was a bright-coloured tablecloth, which was covered with a lace runner. The lace also covered the bottom of some of the wooden boxes that were used to create a showcase. In some cases it hung over the front, making an attractive-looking border and reminding me of the way in which glass cabinets and kitchen cupboards were decorated in many Turkish homes I visited in the Netherlands. Above the table at which we sat, a massive lamp covered with lace hung from the ceiling. The metal saucer, from which we ate a piece of cake, was also covered by a small piece of plastic lace, as were some of the Turkish tea glasses on the windowsill. Alpay explained that it was an idea she got from visiting a Turkish rural family, in which the woman presented her tea in that fashion. Alpay expressed her enthusiasm for this, by her account, very creative way of making something out of virtually nothing. She believed this creativeness to be typical for the rural women who are, in her words, more pure and less spoiled by modern consumer culture.

This statement is a clear illustration of Alpay's double relationship with this consumer culture. On the one hand she is evidently part of, and contributor to it, as she is in the business of selling consumer goods. On the other hand, she uses a very common train of thinking in which consumer culture is seen as diminishing authenticity, a critique that, in the academic world, was most strongly voiced by Adorno and Horkheimer (2000[1944]). On yet another hand, her company tries to sell products with an aura of authenticity and thus commodifies this authenticity. She needs the story that connects her plastic lace to the women of the Anatolian heartland in order to sell her product.

Even though what is referred to as Turkish lace here, is a completely different object from what is encountered in Turkish-Dutch houses, some of the connotations are strikingly similar. Especially the connotations of Turkishness, authenticity and tradition in this setting are shared with the Turkish women discussed before. A cynic might say that these connotations are appropriated, even annexed out of their original context in the quest for profit. I would suggest another explanation. In addition to the polysemic meaning of objects that different authors have brought under our attention, we must not lose sight of the social fabric within which this polysemicity takes shape. Within societies, some meanings gain an almost incombattable pervasiveness, even though different people appropriate these meanings differently in their lives and practices. This makes it insufficient to testify merely to the occurrence of polysemicity. Some meanings are more constant or become symbols themselves by means of their polysemic meaning.

In Haarlem (a city in the Netherlands), on a day

of casual shopping, I noticed another commercial setting in which a sense of 'Turkishness' was constructed. The shop was called *Ottomania*, referring to the Ottoman Empire, an empire of which Turkey is usually seen as the inheriting state. The shop looked luxurious and bright. It had a decor that seemed eager to appeal to the Dutch trendy middle class, rather than to the Turkish population that also lives in the city. This was also reflected in the visitors I observed during my visit, as none of them were Turkish. On display were objects that I recognized as Turkish, both from my own visit to Turkey and from my visit to the Woonkaravaan. Hardly any of them were similar to objects in the import export or impex shops run by Turks, or in the houses of Turkish families I visited. And the selection was also different from what was on display at the Woonkaravaan, showing more handmade objects and a sense of Ottoman splendour and archaic authenticity. Strikingly absent were any plastic products, including Alpay's best-selling plastic lace. What I did see, however, and much to my surprise, were the same items of needlework, or oya's, that were attached to the scarves sold by Özlem's neighbours. The borders were presented in such different manners and to different purposes that they were hardly recognizable as the same thing. They were sold separately as strings, to be used in home decoration, for example as accessories in curtains. The latter were, in line with everything else on display, made of natural fabrics, rather than of the synthetic fabrics with which the windows of Turkish houses in the Netherlands are often dressed.

When comparing Ottomania with the Woonkaravaan, although they share the quest for objects with connotations of authenticity, it is apparent that they are conceived in very different manners. In the latter, the mass-produced, such as plastic lace, is constructed and displayed as more authentic, as it is supposed to be closer to everyday life and induces a feeling of nostalgia for one's own past or a different, more exotic country. Mass production and consumption are part and parcel of these imagined worlds. In Ottomania, on the other hand, there is a search for authenticity in 'the real thing', defined in opposition to mass production and consumption as handmade, made of natural materials, and with a long history. In both cases, however, the products are placed in a very similar context and had more to do with trendy Dutch middle-class taste than with Turkey or houses of Turkish families in the Netherlands. Both commercial spaces, moreover, produce meanings about those objects that Turks usually, with or without pride, call their own. In addition, although the objects are very different, hand-made needlework versus plastic mass-produced lace, the meanings associated with them are similar. While Schneider (1994) describes synthetic fabrics as stigmatised as inauthentic and belonging to the lower middle class, the Woonkaravaan shows how a plastic version of a certain cloth – lace – can also become labelled as authentic and fit for 'sophisticated' consumers.

Both companies also capitalize, in different ways, on an imagined Orient. It is interesting to see that, although the structure of Orientalism has remained rather similar to what Edward Said described in 1978, being, in short, a practice of othering in which the other both appals and attracts (see also Baumann 2005), it is connected to different visualizations and commodifications. The most familiar is a lavishly decorated style, with dark colours, gold and other metals and abundant patterns that mostly Moroccan shops cater to in the context of the Netherlands. Both the Woonkaravaan and Ottomania search for a brighter Oriental style. Clearly, visualizations of the imagined Orient are more dynamic than the underlying structure of Orientalism, as Said already noted. This is not due primarily to the changes in fashion in the 'Orient' itself, but more to changes in the countries of the 'Occident'. This illustrates again the fact that Orientalism is not a product of the East or a reflection of it, but a product of the West. The Oriental other is shaped by the West and by the image it has of itself and therefore of the other. In various critiques on the work of Said it was claimed that Orientalism could not be regarded as a mere ally to economic imperialism. The desires and fears for the other in the West, plays its principal role within the West itself (see for example Macfie 2002; Roodenburg 2003).

Does this commodification reach back to the private sphere of Turkish families in the Netherlands? As the two shops target a middle-class Dutch audience, this cannot be traced directly. However, Turks in the Netherlands are indirectly confronted with the new meanings and functions that are attributed to 'Turkish' objects such as the lace that is central to this article. In both shops changes in function are important vehicles for changing meaning. Although women in Turkey may use the plastic lace for a variety of purposes, the most common purpose is as doilies. When Alpay showed the lamp made of plastic lace to Turkish friends of her parents, they, at first, did not even recognize it as Turkish, followed by a sense of recognition, after which they touched it up and then, as if it was something polluted or weird, let it go again. Apparently, they strongly connected object with purpose, which did not give much space for flexibility. In Alpay's account this is a bodily experience. Much of our experiences in daily life are lived not by the conscious brain, but by the body that moves through and perceives the material environment with all the different senses. The material here is not just a passive receiver of meanings, but interacts with and has an effect on human bodies as well.

In contrast to the older friends of her parents, younger acquaintances were enthusiastic according to Alpay. She described a Turkish second-generation girl as her 'biggest fan'. These youngsters think it is fabulous that something Turkish, that they are used to equate with 'non-modern', can become modern and fashionable by placing it in another context. In contrast to their parents, they have no problem with the changes in use. They want to express a Turkish identity without being unfashionable and traditional. Changing the use of objects is a means to this end. Hülya, the daughter of Özlem from the beginning of this article showed the same inclination when she told me that a bridal chest was the only Turkish thing that would enter her house, but used as a coffee table. Thus meanings produced through commodification may directly or indirectly re-enter the houses of Turkish people in the Netherlands and in Turkey.

This shows how the habitus, or a set of embodied repertoires of practices, is never automatically transferred from generation to generation. Children of immigrants, who grew up in the Netherlands, have different experiences in childhood from their parents. This may be an explanation for the fact that the knowledge they have of cultural customs is less habitus-like and more conscious. In addition, the knowledge of the cultural repertoires of their parents is added to the knowledge of other cultural repertoires, most notably those of their country of residence. This consciousness puts them in the position to strategically manipulate identities and use the meanings produced around objects in the process of commodification. They are able to opt for a more symbolic or strategic variant of ethnicity as described by Gans (1979, 1994). The attribution of all changes in decorating and other practices to a second-generation status should, however, be avoided. In all families, also those who never migrate, there are great changes between generations.

Lace in the immigration setting of the Netherlands moves from a self-evident element of the material and ritual landscape, to something that helps constitute the distinctness of Turkish identity. In this setting, lace becomes a mediator of this identity towards outsiders. And therefore it must enter into the public realm, as becomes clear in the following two sections.

Organizations: Between Art and Tradition

According to Alkanlar, Turkish houses should be seen as treasure chests hiding marvellous artistic expressions. He is a member of an organization called Sanart, a combination of the English word 'art' and the Turkish word for art, *sanat*. Sanart works to promote Turkish art in Dutch society. While doing this, it focuses on the 'art' made by common Turks rather than the high-brow art made by professional artists. Primary examples are the textile-based handicrafts of women. But, though never realized, Turkish food was also considered by the organization as something that could be exhibited in much the same way as paintings by Picasso and Rembrandt. By defining particular cultural expressions as art, they become almost consequently part of the public sphere. They need to be shown to the public, exhibited and thereby celebrated. This was what happened during the two editions of the Göz Nuru Festivali in the years 2000 and 2001. Both festivals consisted of two parts: a competition for which seven hundred objects were sent in by amateur artists, and a festival weekend. The emphasis was on traditional arts, most notably textile arts. All objects were judged by a jury and exhibited during the festival weekend. During the weekend there were also exhibitions of professional artists with a Turkish background living in the Netherlands. In addition, there was a programme of lectures, workshops and demonstrations.

The organization Siri Sunna also operates in the field of Turkish art and handicrafts. This organization, which is operated and founded by Van Onna, takes an entirely different angle. Rather than celebrating the lace making practices of Turkish women, Van Onna tries to redirect these practices into something that better fits into her view of art, which stresses individual creativity and lack of function aside from beauty. This is a conception of art that is dominant in the Western world. Under the name *Zanaat*, Turkish for (handi)craft or trade, she organized a ceramics course for Turkish women, whose needlework practices it aimed at 'transforming'. These, in contrast with Sanart, were not considered as art, but as work, since Turkish women, according to Van Onna, have not learned to employ free time in a suitable manner. When the work is done, they take up the needlework and again occupy themselves with something useful. During the course the participants, according to Van Onna, constantly wanted to go back to making vases, cups or bowls, or other things with some sort of practical purpose. The teacher, a Turkish professional ceramist of urban background living in the Netherlands, tried to convince his students to make objects that were not functional, but solely creative. He also tried to divert them away from techniques that would lead to routine in their work. In the evaluation brochure he writes:

> With the standard techniques they lapse into a certain routine. Then you can no longer speak of a certain uniqueness and replicas are the result. For example, they looked at what was present in the ceramics atelier and copied that. You also see this in the lace making, where copying is taught. That is also a style but it is not unique. Instead, I want the individual to create the technique and aesthetics for themselves. I wanted them to show something of themselves (Siri Sunna 2003: 23, my translation).

Later in the evaluation, he claimed that even though women had reduced the distance towards art, they still seem 'stuck' within the functional. Taskin saw this 'lack of individuality' as the result of 'brainwashing'. According to him, by removing this layer the individual character is allowed to surface.

At the basis of the Zanaat project lies a modernist understanding of art, in which art is individual and creative, an understanding which stands in contrast to the repetition, functionality and emphasis on technique that is considered part of the lace making practice. This stands out against Sanart, as this organization tries to define 'folk art' and handicraft as art that deserves a place in the spotlight. The names themselves are interesting as well. *Zanaat* in Turkish roughly refers to handicrafts, whereas *sanat* refers to art, which can be both traditional and modern. The Zanaat project emphasizes the non-art qualities of the objects Turkish women make. Sanart, on the other hand, not only emphasizes the art-character of these objects, but also, with the introduction of the 'r', making a combination of the English 'art' and the Turkish 'sanat', tries to overcome the gap between a Western conception of art, and a Turkish conception which includes the traditional art made by craftsmen and -women.

Bringing the Domestic into the Public: Festivalising a Domestic Practice

The Göz Nuru Festivali mentioned before did something else aside from positioning itself in a debate on art, authenticity and tradition. It moved something that was usually confined within the privacy of the house into the public sphere. It is part of a process of 'museumization' (Rooijakkers 2000). The contents of Turkish bridal chests were brought within the reach of the public gaze. It is a crucial moment within biography, as the movement of objects from the private sphere of the house to a museum setting alters the meaning completely (Appadurai 1986).

The Göz Nuru Festivali does not stand alone in this act of museumization of Turkish material practices. On the 22nd of May, 2004, I walked towards the building of Milli Gorus[7] on the Jurrienstraat in Deventer, where a Turkey festival was announced. On the square in front of the building were a number of activities, and stalls with food and drinks. After having looked around for a little while on the square that held about thirty mostly Turkish people, my companion and I were approached by a girl who offered to give us a tour. After a photo exhibition we entered a room that was made into an exhibition space. First we were lead to the right-hand side, where a sign read 'bridal room mother'. A bedroom on the day of the showing of the bridal outfit was represented here, as we were told. This 'showing' is one of the rituals that often precede marriage for a Turkish woman, together with the henna night, even though it is now less common. The centre piece of the room was a bed covered with a shiny blue blanket; pink cushions made of satin fabric which was folded to make small squares; blankets with colourful cross-stitches; a patchwork blanket; a long head pillow stretching the whole width of the bed; and a cross-stitched border with lace edging that hung to the ground and removed the structure of the bed itself from sight. In a cupboard there were piles of blankets, pillow covers, and headscarves, all beautifully decorated. On the windowsill was a cactus made out of green fabric, in front of the window two glass balls with crocheting around it. This fashion supposedly started in the Netherlands and Germany and was then transported to Turkey (Hasirci 2001). Striking was also the big television on a wooden table in the corner with a lace doily on top.

In the other corner of the room there was a similar set-up. It was less prominent than the former and it lacked the benefit of windows letting light in. Here the accompanying text read: 'daughters' bridal room anno 2004'. We were explained that the items in this

Ill. 2: 'Bridal room mother' display at Turkey Festival, Deventer, 2004. (Photo by the author.)

room were not all handmade, in particular the bed set, which had lace borders and looked very decorative. Our guide seemed to have a bit of trouble in deciding what exactly it was that made this room modern. The fact that some of the towels and doilies were handmade, but not all of them, appeared to be the decisive difference to her.

The 'mother', who was represented by the bridal room, is envisioned as more traditional and also closer to a supposed core of the cultural custom in Turkey. She makes everything herself, whereas the represented 'daughter' is a shopper as well as a craftsperson. Also the daughter has activities outside of the house, limiting her time for hand working, thereby combining something perceived as traditional and Turkish with something perceived as modern and Western. The room of the mother is given the central position, it is portrayed as something belonging to history, whereas the room of the daughter positions her as both a 'good Turkish and Islamic woman' but also as a modern, capable member of the Dutch society.

Conclusion

In the above I have discussed several pieces of fieldwork material surrounding lace and needlework. This selection was not intended to tell the whole story about Turkish lace or lace-like products, but serves to show how different actors and contexts are involved in the production of meaning around it.

Objects and the production of meaning have specific geographies. This helps us to think about the way in which the spatial interacts with the social. The house, the open-air festival and the shop are different kinds of spaces and, as such, affect agency differently.

First of all, ethnic meanings are not only produced by members of an ethnic community, but also by business entrepreneurs and their designers and marketers. The former may claim to be the true 'knowers' of the meanings of an object that they claim for their ethnic identity, but, from an academic perspective, there is no reason to give them a privileged position or see them as more authoritative. There is no essential meaning of objects, only different meanings produced by different actors. It is therefore relevant to find out whether and how these different processes of meaning production confront and interact with each other and are mutually appropriated.

Secondly, it illustrates the different processes of commodification that cut across the production of meanings. Commodification is sometimes presented as a singular process. However, the above shows that similar objects are part of very different processes of commodification and thus of meaning production. Commodification is rarely restricted to the exchange of use value for money. In the majority of cases something else is traded, namely symbolic value, which varies according to the different processes of commodification. Ethnicity and its icons cannot be seen apart from the capitalist system. An essentialist treatment of ethnicity would be inclined to keep commodified things, especially if this commodification does not involve an ethnic circuit, out of the analysis. However, rather than diminishing the ethnic meaning it may also be seen as enhancing it, which is reflected in the fact that the consumer finds it attractive because of the added symbolic value.

An ethnic meaning may arise out of a circuit of shops and customers that are given the same ethnic label. The Turkish import and export shops that cater mostly to Turkish and Moroccan customers who live in the same neighbourhood as where they are located may be seen in this light. The selling of headscarves in the privacy of Turkish houses, to friends, relatives and acquaintances is another case in which ethnic meaning arises out of the specific ethnic circuit involved.

On the other hand, as the Woonkaravaan and Ottomania do, products can be intentionally marketed as ethnic within a non-ethnic shopping circuit. This meaning may or may not be accepted by the group whose ethnicity is involved, but they are not the ones targeted as possible consumers. 'Their' ethnic identity is produced and commodified without them having a real say in it. They share the field with consumers of all sorts. This commodification of tradition and identity means that sellers of objects become more and more important in shaping and giving meaning to these objects, and that ethnic members become consumers, appropriating ethnically-laden products, even as they are simultaneously producers of meaning.

And, thirdly, different forms of authenticity figure within the different settings. Commodification, rather than diminishing authenticity, has a large role in creating and increasing authentic meaning. Are the doilies sold in impex shops less attractive because they are not handmade? Certainly not to Özlem. She prefers the bought doilies, that are more fashionable in the Turkish circuit of family and friends in which she operates, over the things getting dusty in her wedding chest, whereas Ottomania connects desirable authenticity with the handmade.

Modernity is another concept that penetrates all the different fieldwork settings in a different manner. Özlem's daughter Hülya defines lace as belonging to Turkish identity and subsequently to the non-modern, as she places modernity in a dichotomous opposition to everything Turkish. The antique chest, on the other hand, she can see as modern. These chests are rarely encountered in houses of Turkish families in the Netherlands and as such do not constitute a 'Turkish mainstream' for her. The Ottomania shop that sells 'traditional old and handmade objects', however, presents the objects in a fashion that locates them within modern, luxurious, fashionable and Western home decoration. The Woonkaravaan turns mass-produced objects with nostalgic associations into camp. Through this process, the old-fashioned becomes hip, fashionable and modern. The

Zanaat project defines the lace making practice as old-fashioned, undesirable and non-modern. It tries to lead Turkish women into the world of modern art. Sanart and the Turkey festival also define lace as traditional and old. By reinventing it, however, as suitable for public display, it connects with a modern custom of musuemization and display. Paradoxically, especially by this museumization, a history of needlework is juxtaposed with a modern present in which this practice has to be preserved, because it is, in fact, archaic.

Notes

1. The appropriate technical name is needlework, however informants refer to it as lace. I use both terms liberally.
2. Names of private informants are pseudonyms; those of professionals are real names.
3. About fifty interviews were held in total, and I have translated the quotations used in this paper.
4. Some people believe it is the task of the mother to prepare a çeyiz for her daughters.
5. Several hours each of those three days.
6. There is a very commonly-used emic dichotomy between closed and open people, the former being more traditional and strict and the latter being more modern and liberal.
7. A Turkish Muslim organization, which operates mosques separate from the State-led Diyanet mosques.

References

Adorno, Theodor W. & Max Horkheimer 2000[1944]: The Culture Industry: Enlightenment as Mass Deception. In: Juliet B. Schor & Douglas B. Holt (eds.), *The Consumer Society Reader*. New York: The New Press.
Appadurai, Arjun 1986: *The Social Life of Things, Commodities in Cultural Perspective*. Cambridge: Cambridge University Press.
Banerjee, Mukulika & Daniel Miller 2003: *The Sari*. Oxford: Berg.
Baumann, Gerd 2005 Grammars of Identity/Alterity: a Structural Approach. In: Gerd Baumann & Andre Gingrich, *Grammars of Identity/Alterity: a Structural Approach*. New York, Oxford: Berghahn Books.
Bourdieu, Pierre 1979: *Algeria 1960, the Disenchantment of the World, the Sense of Honour, the Kabyle House or the World Reversed*. Cambridge: Cambridge University Press.
Bourdieu, Pierre 1984[1979]: *Distinction, a Social Critique of the Judgement of Taste*. London: Routledge.
Butler, Judith 1990: *Gender Trouble: Feminism and the Subversion of Identity*. New York: Routledge.
Cohen, Anthony P. 1985: *The Symbolic Construction of Community*. London: Routledge.
Gans, Herbert J. 1979: Symbolic Ethnicity, the Future of Ethnic Groups and Cultures in America. *Ethnic and Racial Studies* 2: 1, 1–20.
Gans, Herbert J, 1994: Symbolic Ethnicity and Symbolic Religiosity: towards a Comparison of Ethnic and Religious Acculturation. *Ethnic and Racial Studies* 17: 4, 577–592.
Hasirci, Nalan 2001: *Nederlandse meubels met een Turks tintje. Stageverslag*. Amsterdam: Meertens Instituut/Vrije Universiteit.
Katschnig-Fasch, Elisabeth 1998: Möblierter Sinn. *Städtische Wohn und Lebensstile*. Vienna: Böhlau.
Macfie, Alexander Lyon 2002: *Orientalism*. Harlow, London: Pearson Education Limited.
Miller, Daniel 1994: *Modernity, an Ethnographic Approach: Dualism and Mass Consumption in Trinidad*. Oxford: Berg.
Miller, Daniel 1998: *A Theory of Shopping*. Cambridge: Polity Press.
Onuk, Taciser 1981: *Kinds of Oyas and Embroidery Techniques*. Ankara: Türk Tarih kurumu basimevi.
Otto, Lene & Lykke L. Pederson 1998: Collecting Oneself, Life Story Objects and Objects of Memory. *Ethnologia Scandinavia* 18, 77–92.
Roodenburg, Herman 2003: Introduction. In: Jan de Jong, Bart Ramakers, Herman Roodenburg, Frits Scholten, Mariët Westermann & Joanna Woodall (eds.), *Het exotische verbeeld, 1550–1950. Boeren en verre volken in de Nederlandse kunst. Nederlands Kunsthistorisch jaarboek 2002, deel 53*. Zwolle: Waanders Uitgevers.
Rooijakkers, Gerard 2000: Mensen en dingen. Materiële cultuur. In: Ton Dekker, Herman Roodenburg & Gerard Rooijakkers (eds.), *Volkscultuur. Een inleiding in de Nederlandse etnologie*. Nijmegen: Sun.
Said, Edward 1978: *Orientalism*. London: Routledge and Kegan Paul.
Schneider, Jane 1994: In and Out of Polyester: Desire, Disdain and Global Fibre Competitions. *Anthropology Today* 10: 4, 2–10.
Siri Sunna, 2003: *Zanaat* (leaflet).
Stone-Ferrier, Linda 1989: Spun Virtue, the Lacework of Folly, and the World wound Upside-down: Seventeenth-century Dutch Depictions of Female Handwork. In: Annette B. Weiner & Jane Schneider (eds.), *Cloth and Human Experience*. Washington, London: Smithsonian Institution Press, pp. 215–242.
Zukin, Sharon 2004: *Point of Purchase. How Shopping Changed American Culture*. New York: Routledge.

Hilje van der Horst is a PhD student at the Meertens Institute, Royal Netherlands Academy of Arts and Sciences and at the Amsterdam School for Social Science Research, University of Amsterdam. She prepares a dissertation on migration and material culture among Turkish migrants and their descendants in the Netherlands. Her articles have appeared in among others Home Cultures and Housing, Theory and Society.
(hilje.van.der.horst@meertens.knaw.nl,
www.meertens.knaw.nl/medewerkers/hilje.van.der.horst/)

HOLLAND ON THE SLIDE
Celebrating the Nation on Television

Stijn Reijnders

Based upon field research, interviews with participants and audience surveys, this paper shows how the Dutch game show *Te Land ter Zee en in de Lucht* is intertwined with other, non-mediated forms of entertainment. For its participants, this programme is part of a wider festive repertoire which celebrates and expresses a group identity. For the audience, the ritualized media use surrounding the programme provides an opportunity to create and experience an imagined, national community.

Keywords: television, nation, audience, participation, media ritual

My husband [aged 33] and I [31] both enjoyed watching as children. They really were cosy evenings … Now the same thing happens with our children. They particularly like the 'jeans-hanging'. When the programme is over, Dad takes off his jeans and they take turns hanging from them. And when Mum puts the washing out they also want to hang from the jeans.[1]

Some television programmes seem to be anchored in the culture of a society: they have been around for so long that their presence has become a part of everyday life. One example of such a programme is *Te Land ter Zee en in de Lucht* ('On Land, at Sea and in the Air'), a game show that has been aired on Dutch television every year since 1971. In *Te Land ter Zee*, contestants are required to slide down a slippery slope in home-made carnival-style carts and ring a bell suspended over the water as quickly as possible, or they have to hang from a pair of jeans for as long as they can.

Te Land ter Zee is not unlike the pan-European *Jeux sans frontières* – a famous television quiz from the 1970s, in which teams from different towns within the EU had to compete by playing games such as running steeplechases or building human pyramids. But whereas *Jeux sans frontières* was focused on a pan-European community (it was initiated by none other than Charles de Gaulle), the format of *Te Land ter Zee* is based on the representation of national stereotypes: the programme is filmed in nostalgic little harbour towns and the Dutch tricolour waves merrily from the stage on which the game is held. On top of this, the programme's title contains a clear reference to the nation's three guardians: the army, the navy and the air force. Within this 'ideological landscape' (Short 1991), viewers are treated to games of a highly folkloric nature, with soft soap, water and handicrafts forming the basic ingredients. Common props such as bales of hay and milk churns should be seen in the same light. In this way, the programme makers try to create a 'traditional Dutch' ambience, a kind of national 'soapbox nostalgia' on television. This image is regularly mirrored in press reviews: the programme is highlighted as 'a mass party', 'a traditional Dutch game', 'a mini-carnival' or 'a pillar of Dutch social handicraft culture'. *Te Land ter Zee* is 'more innocent than cat-bludgeoning, eel-pulling or dwarf-throwing [all once practised in the Netherlands], but just as much a popular entertainment and folk tradition'.[2]

While most traditional game shows such as *Jeux sans frontières* have disappeared from television, *Te Land ter Zee* has retained its popularity for more than thirty years. Hundreds of candidates apply to take part in the show each year. They devote all their free time and creativity to building carts, only to see them crash within seconds in front of the camera. Both the audiences that flock to the recordings and the viewers at home clearly love this mixture of creativity and destruction; in terms of ratings, *Te Land ter Zee* has long been one of the peak performers in the Dutch summer television season.

How can we explain the continuing popularity of this nostalgic, seemingly old-fashioned game show? In this paper, the significance of *Te Land ter Zee* is not explained by elaborating further on the precise format of the show or, in the words of anthropologist Don Handelman (1998), by analysing this 'event' from the 'internal logic' of its design. Instead, focus is on the role of the participants and of the audience, which makes the show 'alive'. Why do candidates apply to take part in such a programme and how do they experience their own participation? Why does the viewing public enjoy watching their experiences? How do themes such as nostalgia and national identity fit in from the perspective of participants and viewers? In an effort to answer these questions, 43 semi-structured in-depth interviews were conducted with randomly selected participants in the 2003 series of *Te Land ter Zee*. In addition, ethnographic fieldwork was conducted during the recording days and existing audience research from the period 1988–2002 was used. Finally, a notice was placed in the TV listings magazine *TrosKompas* asking viewers for their opinion of the programme. This generated 39 letters.[3]

The Annual Ritual

Most participants in the show come from outside the big cities; provincial villages are a fertile recruiting ground for *Te Land ter Zee*. At least 300–400 applications are received from these areas each year. And they tend to come from people with a remarkable homogeneous social background. The vast majority of participants in the programmes are whites, aged between 18 and 35, who have a vocational qualification or are still studying. Just over three-quarters are men. Most participants are groups of students, friends or work colleagues.[4]

The participants usually build their machines on weekday evenings or at weekends. All in all, completing the average cart takes some 200–300 hours of work, 100–200 euros spent on materials – in other words a substantial investment in time and money. While it is true that there are prizes to be won, the chances of doing so are relatively small. What do the contestants get out of taking part, then? What is the added value of being a contestant on *Te Land ter Zee*? From the interviews, it seems that most participants regard the show first and foremost as an ideal opportunity to come together and to present their own group to the outside world. Roughly speaking, the participation process can be divided into four phases: group bonding, competition, display and remembrance.

In the weeks leading up to the day of the recording, the members of the team meet repeatedly in garages, old warehouses or workshops. These meetings are of a highly festive nature. Ruminations about the ideal distribution of loads across axles are lubricated with music and drinks. One of the interviewees puts it this way:

> The building's what it's all about isn't it? ... That's the fun of it. And we really do test [the cart]. He lives next to the [river] Maas. We've even built our own launching site there. [It is] a lot of fun and a little bit of work.

Another participant explains:

It's not work all the time, you know. It's social … With a cup of coffee, with a beer … Yeah, that's fun … It's just … the looking forward to it. That's what's fun about it … It's guiding, helping and supporting one another.

Building the carts encourages group bonding. Some people are invited, others are not. During the building process people take on fixed roles: the women often work on the painting and decking-out, for instance, whereas the men are generally more concerned with the technical side. It may also be that roles are allocated based upon the individual group members' jobs, with notions of professional pride coming into play. Participants openly acknowledge that working together has a bonding effect. Student associations and debating societies, for example, regard taking part in *Te Land ter Zee* as a good way of strengthening the 'club' feeling. Contestants who work together in normal life even describe taking part as a staff outing aimed at team-building.

After three or four weeks of preparation, along comes the day of the recording. The contestants have to report to the location early in the morning, where the carts are then lined up. The rest of the morning is spent with organizational preparations. In fact, the participants are simply left waiting by their creations from half past seven in the morning until at least one o'clock. To kill the time, they wander around, look at the other carts or chat with their opponents. Others ward off boredom with beer and barbecues.

In the midst of these spontaneous festivities backstage the group process goes through another stage: the participants are no longer isolated in their separate groups, they come in contact with the other teams. Although these contacts are amiable, there is certainly differentiation and rivalry between the various teams. Contestants uphold the honour of their own teams by laughing at the others or boasting about their own carts. This competition is particularly strong between groups with something in common. One participant from a local group of friends says that there was another group 'from the neighbourhood' taking part:

But they all had yellow shirts on. So we decided, OK, we'll put on pink shirts. Then we could shout at them: 'Yellow's a gay colour!' With those pink shirts on, just to compete a bit …

A member of a student association describes a similar experience:

There was also a [student] team from Nijmegen, rowers. They were stuck-up, arrogant snobs. They had all plenty of talk, but in the end they sank straight away … They said about [our club] shirts: 'Ha ha, what a feeble slogan.' It wasn't really serious or that, but just having a bit of a laugh at each other. Healthy competition, that's what I'd call it. But you always get that with students, between towns and that. Every student town has a bit of its own character …

By wearing special clothes, and by ridiculing the clothing or performance of others, these groups embark upon a game of honour and shame in which their own pride is the key. In other words, there is a competitive battle to stand out: participation defines groups, but also binds them. Once recording actually starts, this competition reaches its high point. By performing when it matters and reaching the bell in one piece, a group can successfully defend its honour.

Once the cameras are rolling, though, the competitive element is already overshadowed by another interest: as soon as the contestants start sliding down the slope they are displaying themselves on stage to an audience of hundreds of spectators and hundreds of thousands of television viewers, as they are well aware. In the interviews many teams openly express how important that is to them: *Te Land ter Zee* provides them with a national stage on which to display their group identity.

The precise effect of this varies from one group to another. Students, for instance, often roll up at the starting line with a cart based on their debating society logo. Groups of friends, on the other hand, frequently display their group identity using local symbols. A group of friends from the province of Friesland, for instance, appeared in a cart drawn by

Ill. 1: A performance of group identity: four farmers' sons in overalls hit the water with a papier-mâché cow. (Photo by the author, Alkmaar 2004.)

Friesian horses. By promoting their own villages or regions contestants not only boost their group identity vis-à-vis the other contestants but can also raise their local status substantially (cf. Syvertsen 2001: 331f).

> It was very important [to win]. It was a big thing in Culemborg. We were on the regional radio. And on cable television, and in the newspaper. Yes, it really was big ... In the first year, even the mayor came down [to our house] to have a look. She was so proud of us that she came here to watch.

Another respondent tells the following story:

> I now know a whole load of people from Te Land ter Zee. And yeah, when you meet them it's always enjoyable ... I find that great. I just had the idea one day and it is grown into something pretty big at the village level.

The fact that there are promotional aspects to taking part in *Te Land ter Zee* is seen perhaps most clearly amongst the colleagues and small companies taking part. For these groups, much of the creativity lies in circumventing the show's ban on advertising. So the staff of a greengrocer's dress up as bananas, local authority officials appear at the start of the competition in a model of a council service counter and employees of a company called Te Strake build an ingenious 'test rocket' – 'testrake(t)' in Dutch. The manager of a children's farm – dressed as a donkey – explains it as follows: 'Of course I'm looking for publicity as well, for the farm, because we survive on sponsorships and gifts and, yes, you just need it.'

Remembrance

Even as one group of participants is still standing, dripping wet, at the water's edge, the cameras are already panning away to the next contestants. For some of those who take part, that is the end of the party. They lick their wounds and, chastened, head for home. Most groups, however, end the day with a meal together at their local pub to look back over the past few weeks and – for the lucky ones – to celebrate their prize. Over the weeks that follow, their participation in *Te Land ter Zee* fades into the background. Yet the programme never disappears completely, and is remembered in various ways.

A few weeks after the recording, the programme is broadcast, providing a good opportunity to look back. Most teams meet that evening to watch television together. Students organize a *Te Land ter Zee* drinks party in the clubroom to show the members of the debating society or association how they performed. Work colleagues video the programme so that they can show it in the canteen the next day. Groups of friends also meet on the evening of the broadcast. Sometimes they meet in somebody's home, but there are also those who get together on a really large scale.

> We hired a pub, De Mulderije. And we all went down to watch it there. We had a big screen. It was actually the Saturday of the Assendelft fair, so it was particularly enjoyable … We called everyone and invited them: 'First we're going to watch *Te Land ter Zee* – all be there at eight – and then we're going to the fair.'

For many groups, the broadcast of *Te Land ter Zee* is a great opportunity to revive the festive mood and to show their performance to friends and family. Another way of doing that is through photographs: many participants have shots of the day on the wall at home. And pictures of *Te Land ter Zee* also grace many a pub, staff canteen and student yearbook. Finally, there is the phenomenon of the *Te Land ter Zee* fan sites: a considerable number of internet home pages have been set up by participants to describe their experiences and show their photographs. These have a twin purpose. On the one hand they act as a digital photograph album for members of the group, but on the other they are one more way to present that group to the rest of the world.[5]

Another, less common, phenomenon is flaunting the cart created for the show. But some participants do take the trouble to repair and display it – in a front garden or clubhouse, for example. In a few cases it even gains a more elaborate use.

> We always begin half-term with a lantern procession for the children. So I said, 'Let's take part' … So we had to completely do up [the cart] … And then, at the end, we burnt it. Ha ha! Yes, we [burnt] it with a glass of beer in our hands. Yes, a sort of tradition or something, I don't know. An official farewell to the thing, actually it was more that.

This example shows how memories of *Te Land ter Zee* can be shaped by showing off the cart, or even by its ritual destruction. The above quote also hints at another, more widespread, pattern. Many contestants do not get together specially for *Te Land ter Zee*, indeed they have known one another for some time as a group and regard taking part in the programme merely as part of a series of group activities. The example cited above is of a group of friends who take part in local festivities, but staff outings or debating society activities are similar in nature. In other words, the programme is part of a broader festive repertoire for many contestants.

Most staff associations, student associations and groups of friends take part in certain events on an annual basis, for example national walks or cycling days. From this perspective of group culture, *Te Land ter Zee* also has the potential to develop into a regular event. Once a team decides to take part more often and the group process is repeated, the programme embeds itself in that team's festive calendar.

One illustration of how *Te Land ter Zee* has been incorporated into an established group-related festive calendar is the sharp increase in the number of carnival associations taking part. During the first decades of the programme, few – if any – such associations entered it. But that has definitely changed in recent years. Interviews with members of these organizations show that they are groups of people who are used to coming together each year to build a carnival float. Roughly speaking, the carnival season begins some time in September, intensifies from mid November, reaches its height during Lent and ends on Ash Wednesday. But the period between then and next September has to be filled somehow. So, just as festivities can be mutually exclusive, they can also reinforce one another (cf. Rooijakkers 2000: 213–217).

> You've spent five months building a carnival float, but during the summer you have nothing… And then along comes [*Te Land ter Zee*] as an alternative. That's just great, it gives you an outlet for your creativity, after all … You already have enthusiastic people, who know how you go about building such a thing … And there are ideas that don't make it to the carnival float. So we say, 'Then we'll use that for Te Land ter Zee.' [6]

For many carnival associations, student associations, groups of friends and colleagues, taking part in *Te Land ter Zee* has evolved into an annual group ritual.

In some cases, though, participation is explicitly a one-off group experience. This phenomenon is typified by the stag parties appearing on *Te Land ter Zee*. You see one in almost every series: an unsuspecting bride and groom-to-be being manhandled by friends into a 'wedding boat' and raucously encouraged to ring the bell. This, in fact, is an example of a classic *rite de passage*, a formalized pattern of behaviour intended to symbolize a transition in social status. Quite apart from displaying a group identity, this is first and foremost about marking and expressing somebody's position – particularly a changing position – within that group (cf. Gennep 1960[1909]).

A Festivity within a Festivity

It is clear that group bonding and the display of group identity play an important role in the participant experience. Yet that is not so in all cases. First, not all the participants emphasize their own group identity in decorating their cart. Some use illustrations of more general national stereotypes like windmills, clogs, blocks of cheese or barrel organs. Other carts are based upon characters or themes taken from television culture. For example, TV heroes like the A-Team, the Flintstones, Bert and Ernie from *Sesame Street* or James Bond.

A second point is the composition of the entries. Not all those who participate in *Te Land ter Zee* enter as groups; a considerable proportion are individuals. These solo participants are rather aloof from the party. For them, the competitive aspect often seems to be more important than the fun part: technical performance and winning are valued more highly than conviviality and the party mood. And some of these individual entrants are real die-hards. They have their own *Te Land ter Zee* workshop at home, take part every year and appear regularly in their local media. Typically, these active individuals are a favourite subject of scorn for the group participants.

> Look, you have some who are total fanatics. I know one who has been entering the same game for 15 years, and always with the same boat. And yes, he really is foaming at the mouth.

Precisely because it lacks irony and playfulness, the serious approach taken by the individuals breaks with the prevailing code of behaviour amongst the groups: "Some people are so serious. I do it for a laugh. It should be fun."

Another striking difference between the solo and the group participants is their attitude towards the organizers. *Te Land ter Zee* is aired by a public broadcasting association, the Televisie Radio Omroep Stichting (TROS). As a rule, the individual entrants have noticeably more affinity with that organization than the groups, a distinction which becomes stronger the more often the individual takes part. This phenomenon is exemplified by the fates of the two best-known solo contestants on *Te Land ter Zee*. Marco Barink, 39 years old, has now been on the programme forty times and, as a result, has become one of its most familiar faces. At first he felt no affinity with the TROS, but that changed as he gradually became one of the programme's regular participants.

> Yes, I'm a member of the TROS … After a couple of years you think, 'Well, you're entering every time, it's on the TROS and I think it's great.' So then, in fact, you can't reconcile that with not being a member.

Perhaps even more remarkable is the career of Johan Vlemmix, 44 years old. He first entered *Te Land ter Zee* in 1978, but after a hundred appearances decided to call it a day.

> I left in '99, a real farewell party. Then, after having been away for a year, they asked me to come back as a judge and starter. I seized the opportunity with both hands. I said, 'That's what I want!' And now I actually work for the programme.

As a regular participant, Johan Vlemmix became so closely involved with the organization that he eventually had no difficulty joining it.

The teams have no particularly close ties with the organization; in fact many of them are frankly critical of the practical organization of *Te Land ter Zee*. They complain about lack of toilets or showers in the contestants' area and question whether tea and coffee could not be provided. The TROS' only concern, it seems, is to create a 'pretty picture'. According to many teams the festive atmosphere comes about not thanks to the organization but in spite of it:

Ill. 2: Backstage, participants kill time with beer and a barbecue. For this group of friends from Bakkeveen, competing in Te Land ter Zee en in de Lucht is part of a wider repertoire of festive activities. (Photo: www.bikkelsite.com, Coevoerden 2002.)

They don't really create the atmosphere. The organization really takes the attitude, OK, we just have to organize things properly. They are actually making a programme. [...] We're the ones who make it into a party.

For the teams, *Te Land ter Zee* is thus not so much a TROS party as a group party: it is all about group togetherness and displaying the group to the outside world. For many entrants, the fact that the programme is organized by the TROS is irrelevant. In some cases, the meaning with which a group imbues the 'party' can even clash with the image of the TROS. There have even been high-spirited attempts to defy the organizers.

We went against it by trying to shock the TROS as much as possible. That was our real aim. The TROS is just such a cosy family channel, we wanted to give them a fright. It's fun, being a bit provocative. [...] The one at the front who was going to jump, was just wearing a G-string. [...] He actually wanted to thumb his nose at Nance [one of the presenters]: it was a G-string with a face on it. Ha ha! When it came to the crunch, the 'nose' didn't stand out much, as the water was a bit cold, of course. Ha ha! [...] It's fun when you see Lexie's backside in shot.

As far as the contestants are concerned *Te Land ter Zee* is definitely their party, and the teams know how to leave a clear mark on the programme. But when push comes to shove, the organization has the last word (cf. Giles 2001). The TROS can decide not to allow particular contestants to take part, to mark down their performances or simply not to broadcast particular sequences. In the occasional, exceptional case they will even abolish a whole game for this purpose. 'Reversing', for instance, was for many years one of the most popular games in the programme: contestants had to complete a circuit in second-hand cars driving backwards. Within a few years, though, the programme developed in a direction that the organization had not envisaged. As the producer put it:

'Reversing' degenerated into one huge ugly mess. I used to have six bodyguards around me, as the contestants were not exactly the most sensitive of individuals. On one occasion about 20 people wanted to sort me out because their cars were found to be defective. The police had to rescue me.[7]

'Reversing' had turned into a party event that was no longer under the organization's control. In other words the festive atmosphere had been appropriated by a group of participants that was not compatible with the cosy image of the TROS and the organization saw no alternative but to abolish it.

The Audience

In the case of game shows such as *Te Land ter Zee*, one can identify two different audiences: spectators and viewers. The spectators, usually no more than a few thousand of them, are physically present at the recording of the programme. Some of them are there as 'supporters' of the contestants. They have come in the same buses and are there to cheer on their own relatives, friends, colleagues or club mates from the sidelines. It is not unusual for them to wear the same clothes, sing club songs or wave banners bearing the emblem of their association. In that respect, these spectators support the group-based rivalry and competition between the participants.

Other spectators are local 'neutrals'. They have read about the recording of the programme in a local newspaper or even just happened upon the event by chance. It is also not uncommon for a recording of *Te Land ter Zee* to form part of a local festival. Many Dutch villages organize a period of several days during the summer when the community comes together to be entertained with drink, music and games. It is easy to incorporate *Te Land ter Zee* into a busy programme of barbecues, processions, musical performances and dances. Within the context of such a local festival, the recording of a game show does not disrupt other, more traditional activities. In fact, the festival-goers move smoothly from playing field to television location and to dance hall.

Finally, there are also spectators who are neither supporters nor locals. They travel specially to the recording locations to watch *Te Land ter Zee* 'in the flesh'. These day-trippers come mainly for the entertainment and spectacle surrounding the recording of the show. They have no special ties with any of the participating groups, but cheer everybody who reaches the bell. It is telling that these spectators often have the strongest affinity with the organizers. They are often TROS members, and may have formed a fan club for the smiling blonde presenter Nance or brought along banners with messages for her male colleague, Bert Kuizinga: 'Bert, there's a banana in your ear!' When there is no affinity with any specific subgroup, a generally festive mood – largely directed by the organizers – seems to dominate.

Supporters, locals and day-trippers all appear prominently in the broadcasts of *Te Land ter Zee*. In that sense they are not merely spectators but also form part of the programme itself. And they in turn regularly address the viewers explicitly, using banners and t-shirts. That audience comes into play when *Te Land ter Zee* is aired as a television programme.

Who watches *Te Land ter Zee* on television? Existing audience research shows that it is particularly popular with two age groups: children and the elderly.[8] Yet it cannot be said that it is a typical programme for either group and, in any case, viewers aged between 12 and 65 still make up more than half of the total audience. On the other hand, there is one age group which is clearly not interested: amongst 20–24 year olds, *Te Land ter Zee* had a market share of only 6 per cent in 2002. As well as age, there is also clear differentiation in terms of educational back-

Ill. 3: Spectators wait for the recordings to begin. The banner hanging from the bridge reads 'Twente class from Vasse' in the dialect of the Twente region. (Photo by the author, Alkmaar 2004.)

ground. In general, the programme's market share declines the higher the educational level of the audience: from 19 per cent of those with a secondary education, to only 9 per cent of graduates. Breakdowns of its ratings by sex, region and political preference produce no significant results. It can be concluded, then, that the television audience for *Te Land ter Zee* contains relatively large proportions of children and the elderly, and that educational background plays some part in its composition. Yet the most striking thing, in fact, is the absence of any pronounced deviation from the television audience as a whole.[9]

Perhaps the question of why people watch would reveal more. To this end a notice was placed in the TV listings magazine *TrosKompas*: 'What do you think of the programme *Te Land ter Zee*? Tell us what you love or hate about the show, and why.' In total, 39 responses were received. These ranged from brief postcards to letters and e-mails several pages long. The vast majority were signed by senior citizens, children or families – a viewer profile which broadly corresponds with the one revealed through the audience research. Despite the huge variety in the responses, there seems to be one overriding reason for watching *Te Land ter Zee*: fun. Viewers described the programme as 'lots of fun', 'a good laugh', and found themselves 'roaring with laughter' or 'in stitches when [the contestants] fell in the water'.

The question which then arises is what the significance of that 'fun' and 'laughter' is. Upon closer examination, it seems that the fun of *Te Land ter Zee* for many viewers comes from the ambiguous combination of admiration for the participants' creativity and the malicious delight experienced when their creative work fails. Viewers said they 'sometimes felt sorry for them when they fell straight into the water [but] also had to laugh'. It was 'funny when they fell [in] the water [but] I [also] like seeing all the homemade converted bicycles'. 'But the fact that they sometimes make it so complicated and then don't make it very far is fun to watch.' Another respondent wrote the following:

> We really enjoy the programme and double up laughing. But sometimes we do also empathize with those who fail. How it must hurt them. It's a shame, all those good designs getting broken. I find the participants really creative. And I do ask myself whether the water they fall into is clean and free of bacteria.

The above selection shows how admiration and malicious delight are inseparable responses for many viewers. The more they admire 'the wonderful designs', the more intense their enjoyment when it all goes wrong. This paradoxical combination of admiration and malicious enjoyment requires a certain degree of identification with the participants. Viewers need to be able to imagine how much work went into building the carts. The fact that all that work is finally sacrificed in a carnival-like atmosphere is what makes them laugh. Identifying with the work, the tension and the cheerful destruction builds a bridge to the contestants: viewers feel involved with the revelry on television and for a moment there is a feeling of solidarity, perhaps even *communitas*. Laughing at them turns into laughing with them. In this way viewing and laughing becomes a kind of harmonic adaptation for the viewers, a way of joining in (cf. Huizinga 1949: 16–18).

Ritualized Media Use

This participation on the part of television viewers can be intensified through ritualized media use, i.e. fixed actions and customs aimed at symbolic participation (Rothenbuhler 1998: 78f). Many of the respondents said they were 'loyal viewers', were 'keen not to miss the programme' and watched 'whenever it was on'. Saturday evening is deliberately set aside for *Te Land ter Zee*. While viewing, people carry out fixed actions: in practice this often boils down to creating a 'festive atmosphere'. They get together as a family or serve drinks: 'we make the programme even more of a happy social event by having tea and biscuits or sweets, so we really enjoy watching it together.' For many viewers, *Te Land ter Zee* makes for a 'really sociable evening: coffee with tasty biscuits [and] then crisps and a drink'.

An important aspect of ritualized media use is repetition. Watching on a regular basis gives rise to fixed patterns of action, which can extend over a period of several years or even decades, finally becoming embedded in the viewer's daily routine. The way this happens varies. For some viewers, for instance, *Te Land ter Zee* is inseparably linked with the annual camping holiday: 'when we're at the camp site every summer [...] it's really enjoyable watching it together'. For another respondent the programme is rooted in memories of childhood and the rituals that were important then: 'when I think of [*Te Land ter Zee*] it reminds me of the old days when I was little. I'd just had my bath and would sit on the sofa in my dressing gown on a Friday evening, as I was allowed to stay up to watch it on television.' In some cases the ritualized media use of the programme even takes on a generational dimension:

> My husband and I have two children, who both like to watch the programme. Indeed, it's a party for them every time [...] and we are still fans too! I'm curious to see whether our children will still enjoy it so much later on, when they're grown up (perhaps with their children?).

In these examples the ritualized media use of *Te Land ter Zee* has developed into a practice passed on from generation to generation. For these viewers the programme's significance lies in the fact that it is part of a shared past, a past that their children need to be 'initiated' into as well. Sharing the ritual 'socializes' the children, as it were, and makes them part of the group culture.

That leaves us with the question of how the audience regards this group culture, or in other words, what social, geographical or temporal boundaries are drawn in this imaginary community. In the audience responses, it is primarily the folk and national stereotypes that recur regularly. The 'national' image of the programme is praised and celebrated. A large proportion of the audience regard the group culture of *Te Land ter Zee* above all as a form of national kinship: 'I find it such a pure, innocent, truly Dutch programme'.

What is this need for national kinship based on? This is not clear from the viewer's responses, though we could point to a fairly general fixation with national identity since the 1970s. Macro political developments such as globalization and large influxes of immigrants are seen by many people as a threat to the national identity (e.g. Hall 1992; Barker 1999). Heated discussions about what 'Dutch values' should be and what immigrants should learn about 'our' culture rage in the press, television and other media. Very probably *Te Land ter Zee* owes part of its popularity to this. This popular entertainment programme offers viewers a simple and powerful picture of what 'Dutch' means. As the nation becomes less strong as a political entity people feel a growing need to strengthen it culturally, e.g. with an uncomplicated celebration of 'Holland Waterland'. And they succeed in doing so: the programmes attract a large, loyal audience who have come to regard *Te Land ter Zee* as a tradition, an intrinsic part of their shared past (cf. Corner 2001):

> What I find so special is that the whole world around us has changed (and how!!), but the general idea of the programme has remained more or less the same.

The type of media use just described applies only to a certain part of the audience, though. Other viewers may see *Te Land ter Zee* in a similar way, but to a lesser extent. Yet there is another group which has a totally different view. According to some of the audience responses received, *Te Land ter Zee* is 'an incredibly stupid programme', an 'eternal repeat' which 'can go straight in the bin'. For some viewers, it evokes 'the taste of brine, of polluted air, that most people hate'. As far as they are concerned, the TROS should not 'milk [the programme] to the last drop', but instead 'put on a good film'.

Clearly, the need for a festivity that binds is not universal. Rather, there is differentiation in public needs. Not all viewers appreciate the humour of *Te Land ter Zee*. And in some viewers' responses that differentiation is outspoken.

> I know that this stuff is supposed to be funny, but [I can't] enjoy what must be humorous to very small children [...] Humour means something

completely different […] Fortunately, as well as interesting programmes there is also enough humour to be seen on TV. Each to his own. For example, we prefer British humour.

This viewer is unable to laugh at *Te Land ter Zee*. In fact, she finds it an inferior humour. Her preference is 'British humour'. This distinction between 'childish humour' and 'British humour' is striking, yet anything but unique. According to a recent sociological survey, Dutch public preferences in this area show a clear distinction between 'popular humour' on the one hand and 'intellectual humour' on the other. And this divide coincides neatly with a social division in educational background (Kuipers 2001: 110–132). Although *Te Land ter Zee* was not covered by that research, the programme displays many of the characteristics which are ascribed to 'popular humour': spontaneity, conviviality, a non-threatening approach and simplicity. In some of the audience responses to it, a similar system of classification is discernible. By dismissing the humour of *Te Land ter Zee* as 'childish', the critical viewer quoted above is refusing to be drawn into the group culture we have described. Just as laughing along with others can serve as one person's form of harmonic adaptation, so can not laughing be somebody else's way of distinction.

Celebrating the Nation

One important factor in the continuity of any game show is the enthusiasm of its participants. Without an active group of contestants, a good production would not only be impossible but also lack the essential festive character, making it a spectacle rather than anything else (MacAloon 1984). The participants in *Te Land ter Zee*, after all, invest a considerable amount of time and money in the show and at first glance appear to gain nothing in return. Yet the interviews reveal that taking part clearly does provide something: a welcome platform for the celebration and display of a group identity within a competitive context. The question is whether *Te Land ter Zee* can continue to fulfil that role. It is quite conceivable that a comparable entertainment show with higher viewing figures might take over that function in the future. The participants in *Te Land ter Zee* seem to attach little value to the background of its producing organization, the TROS, or to its significance for the viewing audience. For them the programme is an attractive, but essentially interchangeable, forum.

For the audience, things are different. Many viewers have made *Te Land ter Zee* an important and recognizable part of their everyday lives. By watching it year in, year out, a ritualized media use centring on participation in the festive atmosphere has evolved. By watching and laughing, one section of the audience feels at home in the group culture being portrayed. As the responses show, that sense of solidarity is strongly 'national' in nature. The public does not identify with the particular group identities they see so much as with the representation of a national identity. Those group identities are important only insofar as they symbolize the national 'unit' *pars pro toto*. Ultimately, for its audience *Te Land ter Zee* serves as an uncomplicated celebration of 'Holland Waterland'.

For the time being, *Te Land ter Zee* has proven its durability. Over a period of more than thirty years, it has continued to serve a set of differing – and sometimes clashing – interests. The programme has become a recurring festive event with a highly ritualized character and an established group of participants. Programmes like it seem to have become an integral part of today's culture, in which the boundaries between the media and everyday life have all but disappeared in practice. For many of its participants, *Te Land ter Zee* is a regular date on their festive calendar, alongside the annual carnival, fair and skiing holiday. Or it forms part of a *rite de passage* like a stag party. For local spectators, the recordings of the programme often form part of a local festival and attending them fits seamlessly into the round of barbecues and performances. Finally, for many television viewers the show forms part of a common national past. Through ritualized media use, at home or on holiday, the festivity on television becomes a festivity in front of the television. In conclusion, then, it can be stated that over the years *Te Land ter Zee* has won itself a permanent place in

Dutch culture. Television entertainment shows like this have become part of wider festive traditions.

Notes

1. The material to this article is based on 43 interviews with participants, 39 viewers' response letters or emails, and one interview with producer Rene Stokvis. All is available for inspection on application to the author.
2. Citations from Dutch newspapers, respectively *De Stem van Dordrecht*, 08.07.1992; *De Gooi- en Eemlander*, 14.06.86; *Elsevier,* 27.07.96 (2x); and *Algemeen Dagblad* 11.09.98.
3. This study forms part of a doctoral research project about the relationship between television entertainment and popular culture, supervised by Professor Liesbeth van Zoonen and Professor Gerard Rooijakkers. At the intersection of media studies and ethnology, I am seeking an answer to the following question: What is the position of contemporary television entertainment within the cultural and historical context of Dutch popular entertainment? This research has been made possible by a scholarship from the Televisie Radio Omroep Stichting (TROS) for research into popular television culture. It is being carried out at the Centre for Popular Culture, part of the Amsterdam School for Communication Research at the Universiteit van Amsterdam (UvA). Thanks are also due to Rene Stokvis, to the students on the 2004 research course in Television Entertainment at the UvA and to all the interviewees and respondents.
4. This profile is based upon content analysis and the interviews.
5. See e.g. http://www.degraaf.nu/; http://www.bikkelsite.com/tltz.htm; http://www.mislukkelingen.nl/te%20land%20ter%20zee%20fotos.htm; http://home.hccnet.nl/jos.van.oijen/druipneuzen/druip-tltz.html; http://home.hetnet.nl/~bpcvanoort/Te%20land%20ter%20zee.htm.
6. Cf. http://home.hetnet.nl/~bpcvanoort/Te%20land%20-ter-%20zee.htm.
7. Excerpt from an interview in Dutch newspaper *Algemeen Dagblad*, 17.07.1996. See also my interview with Rene Stokvis, producer of *Te Land ter Zee*.
8. The market shares in the age groups 6–8 and 65+ were, respectively, 52 per cent and 17 per cent in 2002, and 50 per cent and 21 per cent in 2001.
9. The figures presented here are taken from audience research conducted by the Stichting KijkOnderzoek (Viewing Research Foundation). Report available for inspection on application to the author.

References

Barker, C. 1999: *Television. Globalization and Cultural Identities*. Buckingham: Open University Press.
Corner, J. 2001: Television and Culture. Duties and Pleasure. In: D. Morley & K. Robins (eds.), *British Cultural Studies*. Oxford: Oxford University Press, pp. 261–272.
Gennep, A. van 1960[1909]: *The Rites of Passage. A Classic Study of Cultural Celebrations*. Chicago: University Press.
Giles, D.C. 2001: Keeping the Public in their Place: Audience Participation in Lifestyle Television Programming. *Discourse & Society* 13, 603–628.
Gouw, J. ter 1871: *De volksvermaken*. Haarlem: Bohn.
Hall, S. 1992: The Question of Cultural Identity. In: S. Hall, D. Held & T. McGrew (eds.), *Modernity and its Futures*. Cambridge: Polity Press, pp. 273–317.
Handelman, D. 1990/1998: *Models and Mirrors. Towards an Anthropology of Public Events*. New York: Berghahn Books.
Huizinga, J. 1949: *Homo Ludens: a Study of the Play-Element in Culture*. London: Kegan Paul, Trench, Trubner.
Kuipers, G. 2001: *Goede humor, slechte smaak. Nederlanders over moppen*. Amsterdam: Boom.
MacAloon, J. (ed.) 1984: *Rite, Drama, Festival, Spectacle: Rehearsals toward a Theory of Cultural Performance*. Philadelphia: Institute for the Study of Human Issues.
Rooijakkers, G. 2000: Vieren en markeren. Feest en ritueel. In: T. Dekker, H. Roodenburg & G. Rooijakkers (eds.), *Volkscultuur. Een inleiding in de Nederlandse etnologie*. Nijmegen: SUN, pp. 173–230.
Rothenbuhler, E.W. 1998: *Ritual Communication. From Everyday Conversation to Mediated Ceremony*. Thousand Oaks, CA: Sage Publications.
Short, J.R. 1991: *Imagined Country. Environment, Culture and Society*. London: Routledge.
Syvertsen, T. 2001: Ordinary People in Extraordinary Circumstances: a Study of Participants in Television Dating Games. *Media, Culture & Society* 23, 319–337.

Stijn Reijnders is Assistant Professor at the University of Amsterdam. His study focuses on the relationship between television entertainment and folklore. What is the position of contemporary television entertainment within the cultural and historical context of (Dutch) popular entertainment? His research project is broken down into three thematic areas: true crime, singing culture and festivity. He has recently published on the former two themes in *Media, Culture & Society* and *European Journal of Cultural Studies*. (S.L.Reijnders@uva.nl)

THE GERMANS AS THE *ALTER EGO* OF THE ENGLISH?
The German Doctor in Eighteenth-Century Debate

Silke Meyer

> This paper investigates a little known aspect of the German national stereotype in England: the German doctor as an ambitious scientist and magical healer. This image was widely spread in the literary, political and medical culture as well as in the commercial advertisements of the late seventeenth and the eighteenth centuries. In terms of national stereotyping, the English regarded the Germans as their allies and near-family relations. The German stereotype functioned as an *alter ego* of the English: the magical qualities were out-sourced from the rational self-image and projected onto the image of the German doctor.
>
> *Keywords*: stereotypes, quacks, newspapers, public opinion, Anglo-German relations

"Make Theodore a Doctor, as he is unfit for any thing else, and ignorance cannot be discovered in that profession."[1] Theodor Mayersbach, the celebrated German doctor an ignorant idler? Surely there is another side to this coin: "I have heard of many more cures performed by Dr. Theodor Mayersbach [...] I have not a doubt but thousands of instances might be found; wherein it would clearly appear that the public hath been greatly advantaged by the labour and skill of the German Doctor."[2]

The case of the German doctor Theodor Mayersbach, who came to London in the 1770s and opened a practice in Berwick Street, Soho, is a masterpiece in public debate and self-promotion. Mayersbach had specialised in the art of urine-casting with considerable success and – according to his detractors – an impressive income of "about one thousand guineas a month".[3] It might have been his economic success which brought Mayersbach to the attention of Dr. John Coakley Lettsom, an eminent London physician, who was particularly doubtful of Mayersbach's diagnoses and their efficiency. The practice of uroscopy was a regular procedure since antiquity but its reputation as a respectable medical method had suffered in the sixteenth and seventeenth centuries (Porter 2000: 116f, 180f). The stock character of a quack without any medical training was described as a "pisse prophet" who lived on his gullible fellow men (Porter 1987: 58, 2000: 181). Still, Mayersbach's clientele included famous names, amongst those the Duke and Duchess of Richmond, Lord Archer and the famous actor David Garrick who swore by the healing powers of the German doctor: "I feel myself at this moment better for your recommendation of Dr Mierbach [sic]."[4]

But Lettsom was not convinced of the accuracy of Mayersbach's judgment and prescriptions. He unmasked the German doctor by publishing anecdotes in newspapers like *The Gazetteer*, the *Public Ledger* and the *Morning Chronicle*. He tested his knowledge by presenting him with an old cow's urine sample, which Mayersbach diagnosed with a violent fever typical for young gentlemen.[5] Lettsom claimed openly that the German doctor was a fraud and he used the stereotype of the German quack to support his argument. Not only was the nationality of Mayersbach mentioned repeatedly but he also ridiculed his accent by writing "dis be not your water", "I tink", "every little ting" and gave him a shaky grammar like "it be no good – she be very bad".[6] Dr. Mayersbach struck back by employing hack writers – maybe his English was indeed not very good – to publish letters in the *Gazetteer* under the names of "The London Spy" and "Sally Spy". In 1776, the anonymous defence tract *The Impostor Detected; or the Physician the greater Cheat: Being a candid Enquiry concerning the Practice of Dr. Mayersbach; commonly known by the Title of The German Doctor* further defends the German doctor and aims to detect the true impostor, the physician Lettsom. This tract also includes a list with the names of Mayersbach's satisfied patients. Furthermore, his clients themselves gave witness of his integrity and wrote letters to the *Gazetteer*, like John Willan on 17 October 1776 or J.S. on 30 October 1776.[7] Thus, the public debate went on in over 100 vituperative letters and articles for the best part of 1776 and 1777, until Mayersbach returned home to Germany as a rich man.

The quarrel of the quacks was rather prominent in London newspapers. *The Gazetteer* was one of the popular morning papers which enjoyed an average circulation of 1 650 copies per day (Black 1987: 16). In this article, the dog-fight between the two doctors introduces a rather unknown aspect of the national stereotype of the German, the German doctor as an ambiguous, but highly successful figure of the English medical market. Next to the German as a sauerkraut-devouring soldier, this image as a quack doctor was wide-spread in England in the late seventeenth and the eighteenth centuries.

The German Doctor in Newspaper Advertisements

Newspaper readers found mentions of the German doctor beyond the debate between Mayersbach and Lettsom. Advertisements in the late seventeenth and the eighteenth centuries contained a large number of medical announcements by all sorts of practitioners, but it is interesting to note that many advertisers claimed to be a High-German or German doctor.[8] The advertisements – their length differs from more than two pages to about four lines – generally followed a similar scheme. Starting off with the address details, the advertiser announced his arrival or a change of address and praised his innovative methods and great skills: "a very expert famous outlandish Doctor, and Citizen of Hamburgh, who is lately arrived here in London and hath brought by Gods blessing a wonderful Art with him". Others simply called themselves a High-German or German doctor, German surgeon or German operator. An extensive list of cured diseases and successful diagnoses followed:

> First, he cures the French Pox, with all its dependants, viz. The Running of the Reins, Pains in the Groin and making of water, Shankers, Buboes, Sandkloat, Spanish Kraagen, Boiles and Scabs about the Head, Holes in the Throat and Neck, and rotting of the Palate and Gristles of the Nose and Gums.[9]

Another "lately arrived and Experienced and most Famous High German Doctor" added to this list:

> This Doctor cureth in an Extraordinary and most easy manner the Morbus Gallicus or French POX with all its Symptoms [...] He has cured abundance when left off by other Doctors as incurable; [...], he promises to cure them in 6 or 7 days, or else desires nothing for his pains, which is as much as to say NO CURE NO MONEY. [ ] He would have no person despair by reason of the long continuance of their Distempers, [...] if Curable he will undertake them, if not he tells you so that you may not be abused by false Pretenders, and will give you such Satisfaction, that you may see what an honest Physitian for Counsel and Physick can perform.

As evidence for their integrity, a list of successful cases was given:

He cured a Child (next door to the Black Horse in Market Lane, near St. James Market) that was born blind in 13 days time. John Howel of the Parish of St. Thomas in the City of Bristol, Aged 72, and Alice Diddal of the Parish of Temple in the said City aged fourscore Years and that they had been Blind 9 years, he restored their sight immediately, and perfectly cured both them and others in 14 days. [...]. This Famous High-German Doctor is now for the Publick Good Setled in the Strand, betwixt St. Clements Church and Temple Bar, at his House at the Sign of the Angel, just over against Essex Street; where the Pictures of Patients, and Manual Operations are over the Door, and where there is a Red Cloth with Stones and Ruptures taken out of the Patients hanging by. And is to be spoken with from 8 in the morning till 11, and from 2 in the afternoon till 8 at night.[10]

The closing lines repeated the German origin as well as the contact details and warned the potential client not to mistake the doctor:

Living at present at the Black Swan in St. Giles's in the Fields, over against Drury-Lane End, where you shall see at Night three Lanthorns with Candles burning in them upon the Belcony. Where he may be spoke with all alone, from Eight of the Clock in the Morning, till Ten at Night, desiring you to be careful for your own benefit not to mistake the place because there is a new person that is lately come over and hath presumed to make use of the Bill and Piece which formerly I did make use of.[11]

Browsing through the medical advertisements dating from 1660 throughout the eighteenth century, we can quickly establish a pattern of recurrent themes: the novelty of the method and the repeated reference to the German origin, list of diseases and the failure of other doctors, evidence through other patients' cases with exact names and the time of their recovery, apparent benevolence in the motto NO CURE NO MONEY, and the defence against quackery by calling others dishonest.

Not all advertisements are as elaborate as the examples presented here. Other aspirants to medical fame simply relied on mentioning their German origin to evoke the image of an omnipotent healer, like the itinerant doctor Christian Krebs who advertised in 1771: "To the public. The German doctor and oculist Christian Krebs, who has performed the many cures in and about Bridgwater [...] has taken up his residence at Mr. Pickard's, Exeter."[12] John Schultim similarly announced in 1762 that

The Famous High-German Operator, liveth at the Three Flower-Pots in Holbourn-Row in Lincolns-Inn-Fields. These are to give Notice, That John Schultim an High-German Physician, and Operator in Chirurgery, who [...] is resolved to continue in this City for some Time, his Art is so noble, and withal so infallible in the Effect, that the same cannot be recommended enough in Writing.[13]

Another advertisement from 1732 does not even give a name but simply refers to "a German":

In Petty-France Westminster, at a house with a black dore and a Red Knocker, between the Sign of the Rose and Crown and Jacobswell, is a German, who hath a Powder which with the blessing of God upon it, [...] If any person of known Integrity will affirm that upon following their directions the cure is not perfected they shall have their Mony returned. Therefore be not u willing to come for help but suspend your Judgment till you have try'd and speak as you find.[14]

Prescriptions were also advertised by associating them with a German art of healing, like a remedy against scurvy called "A Book of Directions and Cures done by that Safe and Successful Medicine Called An Herculeon Antidote, or the German Golden Elixir", which was advertised as healing "most violent Distempers [...] as stoppages, obstructions, raising vapours that causes Swimming and Fumes in the Head, Dimness of Sight; Deafness, and Drowsiness which make the body dull and heavy; and alters the complexion". For purchases, the advertiser gives clear directions: "Mistake me not, the Sign is fastened to the Wall of the House, there is no other German Operator in that Street".[15]

Foreign practitioners must have been indeed so successful that their English colleagues felt the need to warn the public:

> A Caution to the Unwary. 'Tis generally acknowledged throughout all Europe, that no Nation has been so fortunate in producing such Eminent Physicians, as this Kingdom of ours, and 'tis as obvious to every Eye, that no Country was ever Pestered with so many ignorant Quacks and Empericks. The Enthusiast in Divinity having no sooner acted his part, and had his Exit, but on the same Stage, from his Shop, enters the Enthusiast in Physick; Yesterday a Taylor, Heel-maker, Barber, Weaver, Rope-Dancer etc. Today per saltum a learned Doctor, able to instruct Esculapius himself [...] for shame my dear Country-men re-assume your Reasons and expose not your bodies and purses to the handling of such illiterate Fellows. [...] But above all, I must caution you against a sort of Vermin (not to be suffered in a Commonwealth) your Fortune-Tellers.[16]

Needless to say that this warning was followed by the English doctor E. Gray announcing his skills and reassuring the reader that he was educated in England: "above thirty Years since Fellow of King-College in Cambridge and above Twenty Physician to K. Charles II at the Golden Ball in Fisher's Alley, over against the Crown Tavern in Salisbury Court in Fleet-Street". In another version of this advertisement, the xenophobic attitude becomes even clearer:

> Nor be ye so irrational as to imagine any thing extraordinary (unless it be ignorance) in a pair of Outlandish Whiskers, though he is so impudent to tell you he has been Physician to 3 Emperours and 9 Kings when in his own Country he durst not give Physick to a Cobbler.[17]

Female practitioners similarly advertised under the label of the German origin:

> To LADIES and All others of the FEMALE SEX. In Arundel-Street, over-against the Kings-Arms-Tavern, near St. Clements-Church in the Strand, where you will see a Red Cloth hang out at the Balconey, with Coagulated Stones taken out of the Bodies of the Female Sex, liveth Ann Laverenst, a German-Gentlewoman, who, Having but very lately Arriv'd in this Kingdom, and so consequently a Stranger, I could not propose a better Method to make myself known, than by this Printed Paper.

She specialised in problems around pregnancy and birth and devoted her skills to cosmetic challenges: "I also drive away all pimples and marks, yellow spots, sun-burns and morphew out of the Face, Hands and Body, without any Mercurial Paints, and render the Face smooth, fair and lovely."[18] The text is illustrated with a spread-eagle holding sword and sceptre, referring to the association of the spread-eagle with the German coats of arms. Two advertisements by male doctors are illustrated with a spread-eagle and another one refers to "the High-German Spread-Eagle hang over the door",[19] functioning as a sign for the German doctor.

In Anne Laverenst's advertisement, two aspects are remarkable. Firstly, without having access to university education, she claims to have her skills inherited and not learned, thus emphasising the unscientific and irrational aspect in her art of healing. Secondly, her tone is rather apologetic. We can conclude from this tone that the amount of quack advertisements must have been so vast that readers were beginning to see them as a nuisance. The *Publick Register* felt the need to announce on 3 January 1741:

> All possible care will be taken to render this pamphlet authentic, useful and entertaining. And whereas one fourth part at least of all the papers that are now extant, is filled with quack advertisements and other impositions on the public; to prevent the like in this, and to give room to matters of more importance, no advertisements will be admitted, but such as relate to books and pamphlets.[20]

Advertising, Newspapers and Public Opinion

Since Jürgen Habermas' studies of the development of the bourgeois public sphere in eighteenth-century England in his influential book *The Structural Transformation of the Public Sphere* (first published in German in 1962), scholars have come to regard the English press and particularly newspapers as the leading media in the development of the public sphere in a rational and enlightened society (Habermas 1990). Neil McKendrick, John Brewer and John H. Plumb furthermore point to consumption as a defining aspect of eighteenth-century society and the role of advertising in the process of creating a "citizen consumer" since the beginning of the eighteenth century (McKendrick, Brewer & Plumb 1982). Newspapers were not limited to political essays, reports on home and foreign affairs and parliamentary news and throughout the eighteenth century, advertising became the economic pillar for most newspapers. From the late seventeenth century, advertisements began to occupy a considerable amount of space in the papers (Black 2001: 60–65, 1987: 51–66; Barker 1998: 97–99), as the *Craftsman* slightly apologetically informed his readers in 1728:

> We hope that none of our readers will take it amiss, that we have of late admitted so great a number of advertisements into this paper; since we can assure them, that we are resolved never to postpone any diverting essays, or any material articles of foreign or domestic news on that account: But as we found that they increase upon us every week (which must be allowed to be of some use to the town as well as profit to us and the Government,) we have put ourselves to a considerable expense by enlarging our paper and widening the columns for that purpose, without encroaching on the entertainment of our readers.

The Gazetteer, one of the two popular morning papers in which Mayersbach and Lettsom exchanged their snides, devoted on 2 January 1776 over half of its four-column front page to advertisements, and of the following three–six pages, 60 per cent were usually occupied by advertisements (Black 1987: 57, 2001: 60–63).

Many newspapers also carried the word 'advertiser' in their names or subtitles; *The Gazetteer's* full name was *The Gazetteer and New Daily Advertiser*.

Newspapers and especially their advertisements were thus widely accessible for the interested reader. For those who did not want to buy the paper, newspapers were laid out in taverns and coffee-houses and other public places. In 1777, the *General Advertiser* and *Morning Intelligencer* recorded a practice that may well have been more general, organised by individuals or by owners or taverns and coffee-houses: "that part of the paper allotted for advertisements […] is daily stuck up in every public place throughout London and Westminster."[21] Advertisements were open to a large audience and catered for the urban moneyed classes as well as for the lower middle and working classes (Barker 1998: 60–61).

Given the prominent role of newspapers in the formation of the public sphere and of the consumer citizen and given the physical dominance of advertisements in those newspapers, we can assume that advertisements contributed to this development as well. Just as essays and articles on home and foreign news shaped the public opinion in the political sphere, advertisement fashioned popular and material culture and influenced the everyday life of the eighteenth-century newspaper readers. *Mist's Weekly Journal*, 22 May 1725, points to the making of consumers as well as to the shaping of consumers' opinions through advertisements:

> there is a great deal of useful learning sometimes to be met with in Advertisements; I look upon mine to a kind of Index of All Arts and Sciences, they contain Advices both from the learned and the unlearned World; Fools and Philosophers may there meet with equal Matter to divert and amuse themselves. – What can be more edifying to a Beau or a Coquet to read of the extraordinary Effects of the right Italian Cream, the finest Cosmetick in the World of the Complexion, or the Vertues of the true Chymical Washballs for the Hands […] many Things which prove of Singular Use and Benefit could never be known to the World by any other Means but this of advertising.

And on 14 February 1736, *Fog's Weekly Journal* praised the reading of advertisements as an almost educational task:

> I look upon them as pieces of domestic intelligence, much more interesting than those paragraphs which our daily historians generally give us under the title of home news [...] the advertisements are filled with matters of great importance, both to the great, vulgar and the small.

There is, however, at least one notable difference between the political pages and the consumer-oriented advertisement columns. Whereas the political pages addressed readers with "political reasoning", just as Habermas describes it in his view of the enlightened and rational culture of public opinion (Habermas 1990: 86–98, 122–133), the advertisement columns praised innovative products of the latest fashion right next to numerous advertisements of German healers with mysterious practices and inexplicable skills. Joseph Addison remarks that "a man that is by no means big enough for the Gazette, may easily creep into the Advertisements; by which means we often see an Apothecary in the same paper of the News with a Plenipotentiary".[22]

Because publishers made their money from selling advertising space and not from subscriptions, advertisements of German doctors had become as much part of the print culture of eighteenth-century society as the announcement of books and other products. Quack advertisements and hand-bills by German doctors littered coffee-houses, were pinned up in the streets and in bookshops and thus found their way into the midst of the public sphere (Forman Cody 1999: 106–108). And in these advertisements, an unexpected juxtaposition of rational and irrational subjects can be found in the opinion-building media of public reasoning. The rational character of enlightened opinion was thus undermined with a stereotype which does not seem to fit into Habermas' bourgeois public sphere of eighteenth-century England.

The German Doctor in Literature, Popular Prints and Politics

The enigmatic character and label of the German doctor was not limited to advertising columns and the medical market. We can find numerous examples in literature and popular prints like caricatures, broadsides and ballads which show that the German doctor has been a stock character since the late seventeenth century. In 1692 Thomas Rymer employs his image in *A Short View of Tragedy* to satirise the scene when love powder is given to Desdemona: "*Nodes, Cataracts, Tumours, Chilblains*, Carnosity, *Shankers*, or any *Cant* in the Bill of an High-German Doctor is as good *fustian Circumstance*, and as likely to charm a Senator's Daughter."[23] In *Peregrine Pickle*, Tobias Smollett describes his German headmaster Keypstick as "an old illiterate German quack, who had formerly practised corn-cutting among the quality, and sold cosmetic washes to the Ladies, together with teeth powders, hair-dyeing liquors, prolific elixirs, and tincture to sweeten their breath".[24] The German doctor became the German professor, "a cloudy metaphysician", in the nineteenth century, amongst them Benjamin Disraeli's scientist Dr. Sievers in *Vivian Grey* (1827) of whom Grey says: "Matter is his great enemy. When you converse with him, you lose all consciousness of this world".[25] Walter Scott's *The Antiquary* (1816) introduces his Dr. Heavysterne of whom we are told he was "a good, honest, pudding-headed German, [...] fond of the mystical, like many of his countrymen".[26] And Thomas Carlyle shows us the German professor as a figure with both angelic and demonic features in his portrait of Diogenes Teufelsdröckh in *Sartor Resartus* (1831):

> Under those thick locks of thine, so long and lank, overlapping roof-wise the gravest face we ever in this world saw, there dwelt a busy brain. In thy eyes too, deep under their shaggy brows, and looking out so still and dreamy, have we not noticed gleams of an ethereal or else diabolic figure? [...] The secrets of man's Life were laid open to thee; thou sawest into the mystery of the Universe, farther than another.[27]

Ill. 1: The Infallible Mountebank or Quack Doctor. Hans Buling, an itinerant medicine vendor selling his wares with the aid of a monkey and a performer dressed as Harlequin. Engraving, around 1670. (Wellcome Library, London.)

But the image of the German doctor was known beyond canonized literature. A broadside shows that the German doctor's magical skills even aspired to heal age-old maladies like the scolding wife. The satirical ballad *The New German Doctor* (1670) praises his powers as remedy for such a Xanthippe: "A Doctor of late; from the Emperor's Court, / A Person of dextrous Skill by report, / hath taken a Chamber in London of late, / And cures scolding Wives at a wonderful rate."[28]

Here, the German doctor indeed performs a miracle. The illustration shows the married couple with a figure in a long coat standing between them. Not unusual for a ballad, there is no connection between text and image; the same image is used for different ballad texts. Another broadside emphasises the supernatural skills of the German doctor who restored a judge back to life after he had suffocated: *The dead brought to life. Being a true and particular account of a rich judge in England who was buried alive in his own cellar ... also how he was restored again to his tender wife, by a High German doctor*. Edinburgh 1780. Broadsides and caricatures satirise the quack doctor who aspires to cure the devil for gold (British Museum Catalogue 1558) and mock mountebanks who advertised their skills on stage, like Hans Buling or Waltho van Claturbank, the name a pseudonym, in the London of the 1670s (BMC 1032, 1033, 1399, 1405, 1406, 1558, 1406). The stage-setting with various instruments and their companion, a zany and in Buling's case a monkey (ill. 1), show the theatrical elements in the representations of the German mountebanks. A common costume, after sketches by Indigo Jones, was a mixture between that of an alchemist and the *tedesco*, the German mercenary soldier of the *commedia dell'arte* (Katritzky 2001: 127–131, 142). Doctors performing to a crowd as if on stage in a theatre were a common site in eighteenth-century England, so common that Tobias Smollett describes the self-defence of a doctor with the words:

> Very likely, you may undervalue me and my medicine, because I don't appear upon a stage of rotten boards, in a shabby velvet coat and tye-periwig, with a foolish fellow in motley, to make you laugh by making wry faces. [...] Take notice, I don't address you in the stile of a mountebank, or a High German doctor; and yet the kingdom is full of mountebanks, empirics, and quacks.[29]

A finely executed version, *The High German Doctor's Speech*, printed for T. Kitchin, at No. 59, Holborn Hill, London, shows Waltho van Claturbank on stage speaking to a bewildered crowd outside a town and praising his wares to potential customers (Ill. 2). In the background, we can see his patient, his injured leg on a block ready to be treated, his zany and a man wearing a fool's cap and playing a musical instrument as well as a case and some flasks on a shelf. In anticipatory irony, the man shown under the stage has a wooden stump instead of his left leg.

The stereotype of the German doctor was also

used in political context. When Queen Anne died without a successor to the throne, the English crown was handed over to the closest Protestant relation, Georg Ludwig von Hannover (1660–1727, King George I after 1714). The English people, influenced by decades of propaganda against Catholicism, welcomed King George I as their Protestant saviour from the Catholic King James II. Eighteenth-century almanacs like Francis Moore's *Vox Stellarum* and John Partridge's *Named Ephemerides* praised George I as "the Darling of Mankind" who saved the English "from popery, French slavery and English traitors". A song sheet, printed in 1714 on the arrival of George I, uses the notion of the German doctor in the title *The German doctor's cure for all diseases*, the first line reveals the identity of this German doctor: "Welcome brave monarch to this happy isle." John Wilmot, Earl of Rochester, published a satirical journal with the title *High German Doctor: A Title importing an Ostentatious Quack, or Pretender to Physick* in which he mocked the opponents of the Protestant Hanoverian King. By the way, the *ex libris* in the British Library copy, probably of the former owner Robert Lawson, very aptly shows a sorcerer in his chamber surrounded by a skull, a snake, a crocodile, some books and pots. The anti-Jacobite journal was printed from 1714 to 1715 until it ended with *The High-German doctor concluded. With a lively representation of our present distempers: the several symptoms explain'd; and a proper cure recommended*. The Jacobites answered back with the same image: an illustrated broadside, executed by and printed for George Bickham with the title *The High-German doctor and the English fool* lists amongst this German doctor's prescriptions: he has a pill that makes the weakest patient strong enough to get out of bed and encounter "Conscience, Death, and the Devil", a plaster that distracts "that predominant Monarchical Distemper", an ointment that makes "their religion subservient to their Interest" and an antidote to rebellion, disloyalty and decayed allegiance. The German doctor thus achieved a considerable fame in eighteenth-century England both in political satire and in popular culture. The figure had become a stock character and national stereotype; for some he

Ill. 2: The High German Doctor's Speech. A quack doctor promoting his wares before an audience of townspeople. Etching, around 1760. (Wellcome Library, London.)

redeemed the English nation from a Catholic monarch, for others he was but a quack.

The Origin of the German Doctor

It is, I think, no coincidence that many miracles in English literature, for instance in Ben Jonson's *The Alchemist*, take place in Wittenberg, the town where the legendary Dr. Faustus was educated. Dr. Faustus provides an archetype for the German doctor, his legend telling us of his insatiable thirst for knowledge beyond human understanding. The story of this German doctor Georg or Johannes Faustus was well known in England even before Christopher Marlowe's play in 1594. The first translation of the Faust legend is said to be a ballad from 1588, and the first edition of the Faust-Book dates back to 1592 (Empson 1987: 92–95). In *The Historie of the dam-

nable life and deserved death of Doctor Iohn Faustus. Newly imprinted [...] according to the true Copie printed at Franckfort (London 1592), the German origin of Faust is made clear right from the beginning of the text: "A Discourse of the most famous Doctor John Faustus of VVittenberg in Germanie, Coniurer, and Necromancer. [...] John Faustus, borne in the town of Rhode, lying in the Province of Weimer in Germany [...] having an Uncle at Wittenberg [...] where he was kept at the Universitie to study divinity". Since the late sixteenth century, the tale of the famous doctor from Wittenberg became most popular in numerous chap-books and ballads. Significantly, his German origin is an essential element of the narrative, and Faust is always introduced with a setting of his national stage. Marlowe refers to the German context in the prologue: "Now is he born, his parents base of stock, in Germany, within a town called Rhodes; of riper years to Wittenberg he went, Whereas his kinsmen chiefly brought him up."[30] A broadside from 1700 with the title *The Just Judgment of God shew'd upon Dr. John Faustus*[31] starts with the lines "At Wertemburgh, a Town in Germany, There I was born and bred of good Degree." Though the writer here has muddled up Wittenberg and Württemberg, the German scene is clearly set. The chap-book *The History of Dr. John Faustus* (London 1750) also starts with the topos of the German origin: "Dr. John Faustus was born in Germany, his father was a poor labouring man." The image of the German sorcerer had indeed become so firmly established that, in 1610, Ben Jonson could refer to his alchemist with the words: "Or, is he a Faustus, / That casteth figures, and can conjure, cures / Plagues, piles, and pox, by the ephemerides, / And holds intelligence with all the bawds / And midwives of three shires!"[32]

Narratives from Germany as a *locus horribilis* further became a literary genre in the English Gothic novel, or, the so-called German Tales, the prime example being Mary Shelley's *Frankenstein or the Modern Prometheus* (1818). Viktor Frankenstein's aspiration to create life originates from his reading of the works of Cornelius Agrippa, Paracelsus and Albertus Magnus, all German scientists famous throughout Europe in the late Middle Ages and the early modern era. Sir Walter Scott makes ironic use of this dark and fantastic image of the German in his introduction to *Waverley* in 1814:

> Again, had my title borne 'Waverley, a Romance from the German' what head so obtuse as not to imagine forth a profligate abbot, an oppressive duke, a secret and mysterious association of Rosycrucians and Illuminati, with all their properties of black cowls, caverns, daggers, electrical machines, trap-doors, and dark-lanterns.[33]

The German tales are topographically not very precise, town and place names are invented as if the mere mentioning of the German names conjured up an image of derelict ruins, baleful mountain ranges and dark forests. Matthew G. Lewis's *The Monk* (1796), a tale of the flight of two lovers, a wandering Jew and a bleeding nun, is situated in Bavaria but his topographical framework remains empty of real descriptions and is used to enhance the uncertainty and pleasures of horror in the reader:

> The castle which stood full in my sight formed an object equally awful and picturesque. Its ponderous Walls tinged by the moon with solemn brightness, its old and partly ruined Towers lifting themselves into the clouds and seeming to frown on the plains around them, its lofty battlements, overgrown with ivy, and folding Gates expanding in horror of the Visionary Inhabitant, made me sensible of a sad and reverential horror.[34]

Functions of National Stereotypes

National stereotypes of the German comprise, next to Sauerkraut, feathered beds and soldiers, a mysterious quality and supernatural ambition of healing incurable diseases. In looking at functions of national stereotypes in general, two purposes stand out. Firstly, stereotypes are used to create order in a complex and multifaceted environment by categorisation and classification. Secondly, they constitute and confirm a self-image by juxtaposing it with the image of the Other (Meyer 2003: 333–356). For England, the second function becomes evident when looking at the many stereotypical images of the French: When the French are depicted as weak and cowardly, effeminate, foppish creatures with nothing on their mind but fashion, extravagance and Catholic superstition, we see, *ex negativo*, the English auto-stereotype as manly and brave, modest and down-to-earth, rational and enlightened.

English and German relations, however, were more complex. Since Monk Bede, chronicles confirmed the close alliance between the Angels, Jutes and Saxons on the continent and the island. His *Historia Ecclesiastica Gentis Anglorum* (731) was often quoted as evidence for a common family tree of the English and the Germans, and in 1605, the antiquary William Camden coined the phrase of "our Cosins the Germans".[35] Especially when contrasted with the hated French nation, the Teutonic origin of the English was raised above all others, as John Hare puts it in his pamphlet *Anti-Normanism* (1642):

> There is no man that understands rightly what an Englishman is, but knows withall that we are a member of the Teutonick Nation, and descend out of Germany; a descent so honourable and happy (if duly considered) as that the like could not have been fetched from any other part of Europe.[36]

Political relations became even closer with the Hanoverian settlement and the personal union between the Hanover Electorate and the English throne in 1714. In the nineteenth century, German romanticism, set in the mythical Rhine landscapes, was well received in England. Again, family relations were emphasised, as we can see in the caption of a lithography (1837) after William Turner showing Ehrenbreitstein (Rhine): "Ode to the Germans – The Spirit of Britannia Invokes across the main, Her Sister Allemannia To burst the Tyrant's chain: By our Kindred blood she cries. Rise, Allemannia, rise" (Blaicher 1994: 114).

When we look at the Faustian German doctor, we note above all the combination of his scientific and magical skills. This blend was sometimes mocked, often admired and taken advantage of, but never detested like French cowardice or French foppery.

The image of the German thus contained qualities foreign to the English, but not ostracized. At the same time, these qualities were much sought after on the medical market and by the consumer citizens McKendrick and others describe. In the self-image of this enlightened and rational consumer, however, there was no room for mystical skills and magical proficiency. These qualities were projected onto the stereotype of the German, a close friend and ally but not quite family. The stereotype of the German thus served as a kind of an *alter ego* for the English self-image. The same argument can be made with regard to the image of the German as a soldier. The military qualities of discipline and relentless strength were characteristics the English approved of and, in various alliances, took advantage of, but essentially, the typical Englishman John Bull was a civilian, a tradesman, not a soldier. His German cousin, however, was benevolently portrayed as a strong, disciplined and brave fighter (Meyer 2003: 166–171), as a children's book tells its readers: "The Germans have always been a manly and warlike nation, nor is there any country in Europe where there are so numerous arises of horses and foot to be raised, if money be not wanting. The inhabitants when well disciplined can bear the long fatigues of war and are very courageous in battle."[37] By projecting generally accepted qualities onto the *alter ego* stereotype, the juxtaposition of the English rational self-image and the German irrational qualities, already encountered in eighteenth-century newspapers, and of the German mercenary and the English civilian can be solved.

Looking at the German doctor, another observation on stereotypes can be confirmed. Stereotypes are part of a *longue durée* and show structural continuity within the history of mentality. The connection between the German and the scientist with a liking for the mystical and supernatural lived from Faust to Frankenstein and beyond. To this day, ambitious malevolent scientists in films are of German origin, a famous example being the James Bond villain Dr. Julius No from the film *Dr No* (1962). And perhaps we can also see the very public debate and opinion about another controversial German scientist in this light. Professor von Hagens' exhibition

"Body Worlds" where he exhibits preserved human bodies to show anatomical structures was received in Germany as in Great Britain with very mixed emotions. While thousands flocked to see the morbid exhibits, criticism was vast. The English press, the voice of public opinion, instinctively compared him to Frankenstein, Hannibal Lecter and Joseph Mengele, the infamous Nazi doctor. And his German nationality is as much of a topos as his medical qualifications, thus a very modern German doctor who, according to Imogen Rourke in *The Observer*, 20 May 2001, still holds a gruesome fascination with the British public:

> Meeting von Hagens [...] is something akin to meeting Hannibal Lecter. Pictures of this German scientist show a bloodless, dour face, shadowed by a Joseph Beuys style hat, but in the flesh von Hagens is surprisingly uncreepy. He has an honest, open face (he smiles, a lot!), a conscientious manner (he answers every question directly, perhaps with too much graphic detail) and yet there is something about those hands (definitely the hands of a sculptor) and the way you wonder if he's sizing you up for dissection.

Notes

1 [John Lettsom,] The New Method of Curing Diseases by inspecting the Urine, as practised by the German Doctor. London 1776, pp. 4f.
2 [Theodor Mayersbach,] The Impostor Detected; or a Physician the greater Cheat: Being a candid Enquiry concerning the Practice of Dr. Mayersbach; commonly known by the Title of The German Doctor. London 1776, p. 45.
3 John Lettsom, *Fugitive Pieces*, quoted after Porter 2000: 180. According to Roy Porter, this comment was written in Lettsom's hand. The collection about Lettsom and Mayersbach is held in the Wellcome Institute for the History of Medicine in London, MS 3246. For the use of this material in relation to the history of quacks in England, see Porter 1987 and 2000: 180–192.
4 *The Letters of David Garrick*, eds. D. Little and G. Hahrl, London 1963, vol. 3, p. 1090.
5 [John Lettsom,] The New Method of Curing Diseases by inspecting the Urine, as practised by the German Doctor. London 1776, pp. 26f.
6 [John Lettsom,] The New Method of Curing Diseases by inspecting the Urine, as practised by the German Doctor. London 1776, p. 29 and *The Gazetteer*, 26 August 1776, reprinted in John Lettsom, Observations Preparatory to the Use of Dr. Myersbach's Medicines, London 1776, p. vif.
7 Reprinted in Lettsom: *Fugitive Pieces*, II, p. 69 and 102, see Porter 2000: 187–190.
8 The British Library holds two collections of medical advertisements (C.112.f.9 and 551.a.32). I have looked at more than 300 advertisements from the late seventeenth and the eighteenth centuries and 61 of them referred to German doctors. Other nationalities mentioned were Italian (4 times), Dutch (4), Belgium (3), and French (1). In 3 cases, advertisements give Dutch and German nationalities simultaneously.
9 British Library C.112.f.9, item 7, item 85 is almost identical.
10 British Library C.112.f.9, item 2.
11 British Library C.112.f.9, item 7.
12 Christian Krebs, *To the public. The German doctor and oculist [...]*, Devon Record Office, Exeter, 9972/Z45.
13 British Library C.112.f.9, item 27.
14 British Library 551.a.32, item 25.
15 British Library C.112.f.9, item 35.
16 British Library C.112.f.9, item 38. Fortune-telling was also a skill associated with German operators, as the booklet *The High German Fortune-Teller. Laying down True Rules & Directions by which Both Men and Women May know their Good and Bad Fortune [...]*, written by the High German Artist, London 1750, shows. Herein, the High German Artist explains how to predict the future, read hands and faces, interpret dreams and find love by reading moles, hair and skin.
17 British Library C.112.f.9, item 39 and 551.aa.32, item 121 and 140.
18 British Library C.112.f.9, item 26 and 551.a.32, item 31, here decorated with a border.
19 British Library C.112.f.9, item 72, 77 and 94.
20 For the dominance of medical advertisements, see Black 2001: 60f, 63, 1987: 53f.
21 *General Advertiser*, 16 August 1777. For other examples, see Barker 1998: 98.
22 Joseph Addison, *The Tatler*, 14 September 1710, no. 224, ed. Donald F. Bond, Oxford 1987, vol. 3, p. 166.
23 Thomas Rymer, A *Short View of Tragedy* (1693), reprint Menston 1970, pp. 70f.
24 Tobias Smollett, *Peregrine Pickle* (1751), ed. James L. Clifford, Oxford 1983, vol. 1, chapt. XII, p. 57.
25 Benjamin Disraeli, *Vivian Grey* (1827), London 1926, p. 424.
26 Sir Walter Scott, *The Antiquary* (1816), London 1893, vol. 1, p. 117.
27 Thomas Carlyle, *Sartor Resartus. The life and opin-*

ions of Herr Teufelsdröckh in three books (1831), ed. Rodger L. Tarr, London and Berkeley 2000, pp. 10f. Teufelsdröckh's nurse, by the way, is called Gretchen.

28 The New German Doctor, or An Infallible Cure for a Scolding Wife, performed by this most excellent Operator, the like was never known in all Ages. To the tune of, Here I love, here I love; or, The English Traveller. British Library, Roxburghe Ballads, vol. 2, part 2, no. 382.
29 Tobias Smollett, *The Life and Adventures of Sir Launcelot Greaves* (1762), ed. Peter Wagner, Harmondsworth 1988, vol. 1, chapt. X, p. 116.
30 Christopher Marlowe, *Dr Faustus* (1604), ed. Roma Gill, London and New York 1989, prologue, pp. 11–14.
31 British Library, Roxburghe Collection, vol. 3, part 2, no. 280f.
32 Ben Jonson, *The Alchemist* (1610), IV, vi. V., pp. 46–50.
33 Sir Walter Scott, *Waverley* (1814), ed. Andrew Hook, Harmondsworth 1980, p. 34.
34 Matthew Gregory Lewis, *The Monk* (1796), ed. James Kinsley and Howard Anderson, Oxford 1980, p. 154.
35 William Camden, *Remains Concerning Britain,* London 1605, reprint 1974, p. 220.
36 John Hare, *Anti-Normanism,* London 1647, p. 3.
37 [Anon,] *The History of All Nations,* London 1771, p. 65.

References

BMC = Frederick Stephens and Mary Dorothy George 1978: *Catalogue of Political and Personal Satires in the British Museum,* 11 vols. London 1870–1954. Reprint London: British Museum.
Barker, Hannah 1998: *Newspapers, Politics, and Public Opinion.* Oxford: Longman.
Black, Jeremy 1987: *The English Press in the Eighteenth Century.* Philadelphia: University of Pennsylvania Press.
Black, Jeremy 2001: *The English Press 1621–1861.* Stroud: Sutton Publishing.
Blaicher, Günther 1994: *Das Deutschlandbild in der englischen Literatur.* Darmstadt: Wissenschaftliche Buchgesellschaft.
Empson, William 1987: *Faust and the Censor. The English Faust-book and Marlowe's Doctor Faustus.* Oxford: Blackwell.
Forman Cody, Lisa 1999: "No Cure, No Money," or the Invisible Hand of Quackery: The Language of Commerce, Credit, and Cash in Eighteenth-Century British Medical Advertisements. *Studies in Eighteenth-Century Culture* 28, 103–123.
Habermas, Jürgen 1990: Strukturwandel der Öffentlichkeit. Untersuchungen zu einer Kategorie der bürgerlichen Gesellschaft. Frankfurt am Main: Suhrkamp.
Katritzky, Peg 2001: Marketing Medicine: the Image of the Early Modern Mountebank. *Renaissance Studies* 15: 2, 121–153.
McKendrick, Neil, John Brewer & John H. Plumb 1982: *The Birth of a Consumer Society: the Commercialization of Eighteenth-Century England.* Bloomington: Indiana University Press.
Meyer, Silke 2003: Die Ikonographie der Nation. National-Stereotype in der englischen Druckgraphik des 18. Jahrhunderts. Münster: Waxmann.
Porter, Roy 1987: "I Think Ye Both Quacks". In: William F. Bynum & Roy Porter (eds.), *Medical Fringe & Medical Orthodoxy 1750 ~ 1850.* London: Croom Helm, pp. 56–78.
Porter, Roy 2000: Quacks. Fakers and Charlatans in English Medicine. Stroud: Tempus.

Silke Meyer is lecturer of European Ethnology at Münster University. Her research interests and publications focus on hero figures, stereotypes, national identity, visual culture and media discourse as well as the culture of credit as part of an economic anthropology.
(meyers@ uni-muenster.de)